AN

EDITED

LIFE

Hardie Grant

QUADRILLE

AN
EDITED
LIFE

Simple Steps to
Streamlining Your Life,
at Work and at Home

Anna Newton

Introduction

If you need someone to hold your hand while you clear out your wardrobe – a task you've been postponing for the last five years – then I'm your girl. If you want to have a look in a friend's diary to see how they organise their shit, then mine's an open book. If you fancy some meditation app recommendations so you can live a life more zen, I have some suggestions up my sleeve. But most importantly, if you need a karaoke partner to do the Sean Paul rap in Blu Cantrell's 'Breathe', look no further.

I'm Anna, a part-time carpool karaoke singer at the weekends and a full-time blogger and organisation freak the rest of the time. I'm a textbook Virgo and thoroughly enjoy reading about the hard-working and efficient tendencies of my star sign with an annoying smugness that drives my other half insane. *Classic Virgo right there*. I've had my blog 'The Anna Edit' since 2010, and although it started off as a chronicle of the large abundance of beauty products and makeup that I was secretly building a fort with at home, it's since turned into a place where I share a bit of everything – from productivity tips to Ryan Gosling memes, and from capsule wardrobe how-tos to dealing with facial hair when you've inherited your dad's genes and look like Tom Selleck if you dodge your razor for too long. It's a pretty varied corner of the internet. Come and say hi sometime.

Although I was a child who enjoyed colour-coordinating her Crayola crayons in her spare time, my personal editing journey began when I lived in East London for three years post-university with my now-husband Mark, in a one-bedroom flat. We basked in our close proximity to Westfield (a retail centre that was shopping nirvana during the week and claustrophobic shopping hell at the weekend), spent £45 on a pack of crackers, chia pudding and hummus crisps at Whole Foods and knew the exact carriage to embark on the central line to conveniently drop us at the foot of the stairs at our destination station. We further revelled in this authentic London experience with a flat that was the size of a postage stamp. We devised our own little space-saving hacks like hiding the ironing board behind the sofa and squashing a vacuum cleaner behind an open door, but after years of a consumer-heavy lifestyle, my new purchases soon began to creep into every empty crevice. The bathroom became a candle-hoarding zone, drawers were overflowing with new bedding, and opening the wardrobe door became a task that should have had its own health-and-safety warning: 'HARD HATS MANDATORY'. Now, being the Virgo that I am, nothing was ever messy, but there was just an overwhelming amount of *stuff*.

An amount that you truly don't realise you have until you move. And isn't that always fun? As we made the journey 50 miles south to Brighton after our time in the big smoke, I still remember moving into our new place lugging a box that said: 'OLD MAKEUP – BOX 3' on the side, much to our new neighbour's amusement.

Thankfully our new home was a little roomier, but as I unpacked the seemingly never-ending pile of boxes, I realised that the majority were full of items that I didn't need, like or even use. A broken iPod Shuffle! A sequin dress from Topshop that made me look like an overstuffed sausage when I tried it on! A university textbook that wasn't just unread, but still had the plastic wrapping intact! The moment I pulled out an egg slicer – don't ask – was the icing on the cake. Cue an afternoon read of Marie Kondo's *The Life-Changing Magic of Tidying*; the bestselling decluttering bible that preaches that we should only hold on to possessions that are either purely functional or give us a feeling of joy when we hold them in our clutches. Fast-forward to a couple of days later and the egg slicer had been removed, along with another five bin bags of complete tat, two bags of items for the clothes bank and a pile of electronic goods for the charity shop. That week my lifestyle did a subtle shift without me even realising, and began to point in the direction towards a scary sounding place – *minimalism*. In the months that followed, not only did our home instantly feel more functional, my brain took a long exhale for the first time in months, giving new ideas a spot to nestle in. It was a truly clichéd 'weight off my shoulders' moment and, with our belongings in order, I found myself being more productive with work and more efficient with my time. We even started to plan our meals ahead and ditched the too-frequent takeaways that were zapping away at our bank accounts. I found myself buying less in general and gravitating towards purchases that fitted with that classic 'quality over quantity' saying. This physical dumping of stuff also meant fewer boxes to unpack. DOUBLE WIN.

Being the 'all or nothing' gal that I am – it's in my star sign, you know? – this feeling quickly became addictive, to the point where my husband was concerned that he'd come home to find that I'd binned the TV remote because it just wasn't bringing me joy. I devoured books, blogs and podcasts on the subject and loved nothing more than throwing shit out. I cleared kitchen cupboards at the weekend, looted our loft for more items to take down to the dump, bullied my mum into downsizing her vase collection (which, in fairness, had got a little out of control and was nearing the 50+ mark) and developed a penchant for PP storage from MUJI. In my eyes I was ticking all the minimalist boxes, but in reality I was living with a capsule wardrobe that only contained seven tops and I never had any clean clothes to wear. I'd become the complete opposite of a hoarder and instead became a bin-bag-filling tyrant, obsessed with lobbing the next load into the tip, to the point that I was parting with things that we actually needed. As I suspiciously eyed up the TV remote, I realised that there had to be a more comfortable middle ground.

Over the next couple of years I devised methods, mantras and editing processes that still sat within a semi-minimalist framework, but didn't act as a strict rulebook like all the texts on the topic that I'd previously read. The TV remote breathed a sigh of relief and the capsule wardrobe became a staple part of my lifestyle without the 'how long can I wear this top for before it grows legs?' aspect.

Minimalism as a term is broad. It covers a whole spectrum of *living with less* beliefs, from only owning possessions that you can squeeze into one suitcase, to halving your collection of 'Now That's What I Call Music' CDs that were about to topple off your shelf anyway. At the strictest end, it can be very prescriptive. I struggled with the whole 'seven shirts' thing, let alone those who set themselves the challenge of a 10-item-only capsule wardrobe. So what I've come to see as the middle ground is to aim for a more *edited* life. It's an ongoing process that embraces imperfections and shrugs off the need for perfectionism, because perfection just doesn't exist unless we're talking about Ryan Gosling.

So welcome to *An Edited Life*. A book crammed full of practical tips I've discovered over the years through my journey from consumer queen to militant thrower-outer to a slightly more chilled neat-freak. By clearing out those dusty possessions and creating daily time-saving habits, you'll be given a bit more space in your brain to deal with everything else that's going on in life. I've read enough of these books to know that they can get a little '*I wake up in the morning and drink a wheatgrass shot in my white linen loungewear before I meditate for 30 minutes and gaze out into the ocean…*' But the intention of this book isn't to intimidate, rather it's to arm you with advice for changes and goals that are doable and achievable, and don't require a sea view and snot-coloured shooters.

Millennial life is pretty nuts. If we're not Instagramming pictures of our food, then we're buying a ridiculous amount of things that we don't need because Facebook suggested it. (And if we're not doing either of those things we're probably off somewhere complaining that millennial life is hard – oh the irony.) There's a lot going on, and with our cupboards bulging, social calendars heaving and our follicles unable to remember the last time we got a haircut, it's time to slow down, take a bit of time for ourselves and take stock. I hope reading this book gives you an excuse to take a weekend for you to do whatever it is that you want to; a Netflix binge or a Sunday roast at the pub with your parents, with a highly competitive game of Scrabble after dessert. I'd love it to give you a motivational kick up the rear, a stirring in your stomach to do all those annoying #adulting errands that you've been putting off for months, or a push to book yourself in for a manicure and lose yourself in trashy magazines for half an hour.

In the past four years I've discovered that life organisation as a broad term is not just about physical stuff. We'll get round to the wardrobe clear-out, but in the context of *An Edited Life*'s aim of sprinkling more good vibes into your day, it's achieved through a combination of decluttering, creating helpful daily habits and shifting your mindset to a more content and purposeful place. Firstly, I suggest working on your daily engagements and carving out a schedule that works for you and allows time for work, responsibilities, self-care and a social life. I know. It sounds MAD, but it's possible. Once you're a diary pro it's time to focus on the work side of things, from deadlines to digital organisation. Then finally, dig into your home and possessions and say goodbye to the unwanted tat that's causing mind and space clutter. By leaving this classical minimalist method as the final step it's more likely that you'll have weakened your hoarder's grip even just a little, and sorted out what you really need to keep for your newly edited life, rather than chucking away things it turns out you really need. Goodbye 'OLD MAKEUP – BOX 3'!

It sounds easy and simple, and that's because it is. The thing to remember is that there is not a 'one size fits all' approach when it comes to organisation, because we're throwing out the rulebook here and burning it on the pile of paperwork that you've had locked up for the past 15 years. *An Edited Life* is going to enable you to sculpt out your own personal routine through applying and adapting strategies from three simple sections that cover life, work and home. Each section features hacks, lists and practical advice to get you started on creating a more organised way of living that's unique to you and your needs as an individual. It's not about doing a complete 180 and begrudgingly binning all your possessions; it's more about tweaking your life and making it a little more streamlined by editing out the things and thoughts that are eating away at the clock. It's about being able to choose an outfit for the day ahead in two minutes, thanks to your handy capsule wardrobe, instead of 20 minutes spent panicking at that mound of clothes on your chair. It's about locking your phone in a drawer for a couple of hours and indulging in a digital detox instead of it being surgically attached to your hand. It's about spending your Sunday watching back-to-back episodes of *RuPaul's Drag Race*, instead of going to the birthday party of your best friend's boyfriend's cousin's (once removed) niece. And not feeling guilty about any of it.

Above all, I hope that reading *An Edited Life* makes you feel good. I hope it provides you with a couple of laughs, a light-hearted look at life organisation, and the tools and tips to have a spring clean of your own, whatever the time of year. Think of it not as a book of commandments to be followed to the letter, but more like your crazy-tidy friend (who actually enjoys hoovering) offering titbits of advice.

This book goes out to all my fellow Monicas out there, as well as those who identify as more of a Phoebe or Rachel. Even if you're already a devoted capsule-wardrobe follower who loves to Bullet Journal, I'm sure there will be some things in here that will help you simplify your life even further. For those who are looking for a bit more guidance when it comes to organisation in all areas of life, then you've come to the right place. There's no judgement here, just tips, tricks and lots of Ryan Gosling references (total Ryan Gosling inclusions in this introduction: three). Get comfy, have a read and say hello to your new, much improved, edited life.

The basics

If you ever feel like you need steering in the
right direction, then here are the basics that
ultimately create the foundations for an
edited life. These eight key beliefs govern all
chapters of the book, and we'll revisit them
time and time again; think of this as your
mission statement/moral compass mash-up.

QUALITY OVER QUANTITY. Always. Aim to live with an edited amount of high-quality possessions and goods that are either used often or add value to your life in some way.

STOP. BUYING. SHIT. In the same vein as the above, make purchases that are based on your needs, instead of wants. TREAT YO' SELF occasionally, but try to unplug from a constantly consuming lifestyle.

PLANNING IS KEY. Not only do well-thought-out plans help to spur us on to think about the bigger picture, they make it easier to structure realistic and attainable goals that, when ticked off, make us feel like we're actually getting stuff done.

NO – THE MAGIC WORD. Know when it's right to carve out time for you and avoid spreading yourself too thin. Respect your schedule and learn when it's best, both physically and mentally, to say no.

A TIDY HOME = A TIDY MIND. If your belongings are in order then there's less chance of procrastination and physical clutter getting in the way of tasks that you actually need to complete.

SLEEP. A LOT. It's amazing what we can achieve when we're fully rested. Aim for eight hours a night if possible. Beyoncé eat your heart out.

BE KIND. Aside from being a nice human, make sure you treat yourself with the love and respect that you deserve. Move more. Eat well. Rest up (yes; I will be banging on a *lot* about sleep).

DO MORE OF WHAT MAKES YOU HAPPY. That's the end goal here. Through tweaking the organisational aspects of your life, work and home, space will appear for you to spend more time doing whatever the hell it is that makes you the happiest.

Before you begin...

Before you get down to the nitty gritty, a couple of things. Don't worry, I'm not going to make you write your thoughts and feelings down Dear Diary style, but I do think that it's a good idea just to have a moment of reflection on where you're currently at right now.

Lock yourself a way for a 10 minute sit-down, or take yourself off for a walk and think about where you're currently at in life, with work and in your home.

What areas of your life do you feel need a shift?

What aspects have you got completely *down*?

Are there some parts that you feel like you should tweak but really can't be arsed?

From my experience it's worth listening to your answers and beginning by working on the elements that you're excited to apply yourself to and returning to those you're not so willing to shift later, when you've got a bit more fire in your belly thanks to the previous positive changes you've made that are making you feel like an absolute BOSS.

With that in mind I suggest utilising this book in two ways. Either flick through in the classic sense from beginning to end, or have a browse of the contents and jump to the section that shouts out to you most. I've laid this book out in the order that I feel it works best as an overall method, but you might interpret it differently. So if it makes sense for you to start with mastering your workspace first and then returning to the start, be my guest. There is no one correct way to organise. At the heart of editing is modification, so seize the chance to have your editor moment à la Ms. Wintour.

And just so we're clear – I'm a child-free, almost 30 year old who works for myself from home and so my experiences with life organisation are going to be very different to those of a working mum of two who heads to an office everyday. I've been a hard-up student who hung on financially thanks to my trusty overdraft and the reduced section of the local Co-op during my University years, so I feel like I've got the backs of the book-smart contingent. However, having never experienced motherhood I understand that some of my suggestions might not be the most practical when you don't even have time to poo in peace. You are superwomen and I have mad respect for you all. Remember, it's all just a phase! I now allow my parents to poop without me peeking around the door. As I've mentioned already – different strokes for different folks and all that – so cherry pick through the pages as you please.

If there's a chapter that you're particularly interested in then make sure to check the **Resources** section at the end of the book for some extra pointers in the right direction. There you will find websites, podcasts and books that I often use as sources of inspiration when I feel like I need to sharpen my sorting skills. On my blog you'll find print-out PDF worksheets covering topics from this book if you fancy yourself a free download or two and want to dig deeper. There's also 2500+ articles on there that span a range of topics and contain links to related articles, videos and channels. Just please don't click back to 2010. It was the year of fake tan. Need I say anymore?

At the end of each chapter you'll find **The Edit** section that summaries where we're at and what's coming next, then at the end of each section - **life**, **work** and **home** - there are checklists to tick off if you're not quite sure where to get started. Right at the back you'll find plans to edit your life over the period of a weekend, a month or three months, so there you'll find how best to fit all the pieces of the puzzle together – whatever the time frame. Feel free to jot down notes, circle sentences, get messy in whatever way you feel you need to for it to stick. Whenever I'm reading I like to highlight pages that I think I might need to return to with tabs or post-its so they're easy to reference later on. If you find a page that you deem post-it worthy then I'm honoured. Thank you.

RIGHT, TIME TO EDIT...

Typically, when we're overwhelmed we often think that in order to feel calm we need to get rid of everything we own. So we dig a bin bag out of the cupboard, curse when we can't find the perforated edge and start throwing items in willy-nilly in the hope that through doing so we will instantly be transported to a place of pure tranquillity that I think only exists in Instagram pictures of horizons. Hey – sometimes it works and I ain't knocking that method, but in order for these new efficient habits and routines to stick, it's important to address brain clutter before actual clutter.

Forget bin bags: we're talking about what comes before you even reach for them, and making sure that when you do get round to reorganising your home, you'll be in the best headspace for it.

Instead of focusing on *stuff*, let's focus on you. Equip yourself with the tools you need to arrange a calendar that doesn't make you feel like you need to breathe into a paper bag when you look at it. Rip open your stack of dusty envelopes and sort your finances out because it's time to crack out the b-word. Oh yes, it's BUDGETING TIME. Self-care might sound like marketing bumf, but it's an important skill that we all need to learn to hone – from allowing ourselves to rest to eliminating unwanted stressors *karate chops away all feelings of anxiety*. Basically, it's time to get your cards in order and nail self-preservation. You've got this...

Sort your diary out

A diary is your life PA and the key to knowing exactly what you need to do at what time and where, so let's make sure you have a solid time-planning structure in place to provide the basic foundations for an edited life.

Can you believe there was a time in our lives when we didn't have calendars? I KNOW. Of course there were the *Dear Diary* electronic planners and *Forever Friends* padlocked notebooks of the nineties, but the chances are that there was a period in your life where you didn't have a written schedule, and even if you did, you weren't a slave to it. Now, I'm not a fan of the latter, but I definitely am of the former. Having a schedule to follow, albeit paper or digital, allows us to be in control of our own timesheets, to chisel out some free hours and, in theory, never miss a meeting, appointment or birthday again – because we all know we feel like a massive flop whenever that happens.

With this in mind, scheduling is the first chapter in this book. It's about creating an organisational framework that's tailored to you, fits with your needs and preferences, and arms you with an empty structure in which to slot your edited life. Without one I can pretty much guarantee that you won't be using your time effectively, and if you are then we're all giving you a round of applause right now because your memory must be record-breaking and I really hope you're putting that skill to good use. A well-formed and clear calendar is the number one organisational tool you can have. The lists, the budgets, the plans, the self-care, the declutters, the daily habits – they are all created because you've put the time in your calendar to get the ball rolling. It sounds deceptively simple, but the root of every chapter in this book can be traced back to the humble diary.

First, why don't you sit down and open up your current calendar? Are you feeling on top of it? GO YOU – feel free to breeze through this section and move on to the next. However, if yours is just an eyeball-aching mess of dates, times and scribbles that you're struggling to decipher because you scrawled them in after one too many wines, then you've come to the right place.

Paper vs. digital

If your diary resembles a piece of children's artwork with script
that even you can't read, or you keep turning up to your dentist
appointment a week early, then it's probably time to face up to the fact
that it's worth starting from scratch because your current method isn't
serving its one true goal, which is keeping you on track. But what do
you choose? Paper or digital? Back in the day I was all about a diary
that I could hold in my hand. I felt like a proper adult, and although
Tipp-Ex became my new best friend, it was quite handy to be able
to turn down on-the-spot invites that I couldn't think of an excuse for
quickly enough off the top of my head, because I '*didn't have my diary
with me*'. I'm a terrible person.

However, three years ago I moved to iCal, the standard calendar app
that comes with all Apple devices. It was a move that I resisted for a
long time (much to the annoyance of my colleagues), but was one that
once completed meant that I was easily able to share my plans with
my managers, parents and husband. I tossed the Tipp-Ex in the bin
and have been able to schedule, reschedule and remove appointments
ever since. For ease of use, flexibility and the fact that I can simply
look at how the rest of my month is panning out in one click, it's now
my preferred method. But whatever your chosen medium, I have some
recommendations up my sleeve for you.

CAN'T DECIDE WHICH ONE TO CHOOSE?

What calendar method
are you currently using?

Paper   Nothing   Digital

Do you manage
to keep it neat?

Do you forget to add
appointments?

Does your schedule change
from week to week?

Do you mind carrying
a notepad with you?

Would sharing your calendar
be helpful for others?

Has the idea of Bullet
Journals ever appealed?

PAPER   **DIGITAL**

PAPER CALENDAR RECOMMENDATIONS:

FOR THE BUSINESS PROFESSIONAL: **MOLESKINE**
My first foray into proper grown-up diaries when I entered the world of work. They'll forever have a special place in my heart and they get a thumbs-up for the large number of colours, sizes and paper layouts available.

FOR LOVERS OF SKANDI-INSPIRED INTERIORS: **APPOINTED**
I'm not sure that diaries get much more chic than these. I enjoy their weekly planner layout the best, although they offer a Filofax-esque set-up too. If you're feeling real fancy you can choose to have your purchase monogrammed.

FOR THOSE WHO LIKE TO SWITCH IT UP YEAR TO YEAR:
PAPERCHASE
The largest offering on the high street with a range of sizes, prints and all sorts of specialised diaries, from food to fitness. Be warned: you will want to buy the rest of the entire range from the print that you buy.

FOR CREATIVES WHO WANT THEIR DIARY TO HAVE COVER APPEAL: **OHH DEER**
If you fancy something quirky that's going to look inviting on your desk, then look no further. No one does weird and wonderful stationery quite like them. If they could turn some of their patterns into wallpaper then that would be fab. THANKS.

FOR THOSE WHO LIKE DETAIL-FOCUSED LAYOUTS: **KIKKI K**
There is a section on their website solely for 'organising'. Need I say anymore? Their selection is simple and minimal and the page layouts well thought-out for various different ways of scheduling. Top marks all round.

CALENDAR APP RECOMMENDATIONS:

FOR THOSE WHO WANT A QUICK, EASY AND FREE OPTION:
OUTLOOK, APPLE CALENDAR, GOOGLE CALENDAR
The most frequently used calendar apps that are all pretty similar and are offered up as standard depending on whether you're an Apple or Microsoft user, and what service provider you use for email.

BUSYCAL (FOR APPLE USERS)

A fully customisable interface where you can also keep on top of to-do lists, set reminders and alarms, and add journal entries or sticky notes. A great option for those who want a one-stop productivity shop.

BLOTTER (FOR MAC USERS)

This isn't the most multi-tasking of the calendar apps, but it's certainly one of the prettiest as it creates a calendar view that blends in with your desktop.

FANTASTICAL (FOR APPLE USERS)

There's a general consensus that this is *the* app for scheduling. It's pricey, but it features everything you need to keep on top of life, from reminders to checklists. One for true organisation freaks with attention to detail.

CLOUDCAL (FOR ANDROID USERS)

The selling point of this app is that each day is represented by a ring that fills with task-specific colours as you add items into your agenda, so it's easy to see at a glance just how busy you're looking each day and what you're up to.

Once you've pinned down your scheduling medium, get to work filling it out.

1   Begin by adding in longer events like holidays, conferences or school breaks.

2   Next, work your way down to the smaller agenda items like recurring meetings, appointments and workout classes.

3   This isn't a to-do list (we'll get to that later): this is about events and plans you've made, so stick to those for now.

I sometimes find that I can get a little too chuffed with my new calendar set-up and end up filling every waking moment with a colour coordinated chunk of time, leaving no actual slots for me to do non-diarised activities like slob on the sofa in a pair of leggings that the waist elastic went on three years ago, or meet up with friends. So stick to high-priority, essential stuff only, and leave out your daily tasks, errands and general to-do lists. Remember, a diary, calendar or schedule – whatever you call it – is there to show you where you'll be and when. That's it. All the other stuff comes under planning, which I save for to-do lists, productivity apps or a notebook. We'll get there, don't worry.

Give your chosen method a test for a month, before checking in to see if it's working for you. Are you forgetting to look at it at least daily? DITCH IT. Do you find it a pain in the arse to make changes to your schedule? GIRL BYE. Are you finding it too time-consuming to keep on top of? LET IT GO. In all these instances, or if it's just not vibing with you, don't be afraid to troubleshoot and start from scratch again. If you're not checking it when you should be, then keep your diary app on your desktop or store your calendar in a prominent spot at your workplace. If making changes means you spend five minutes fiddling around on your phone or have to physically cross out meetings, which makes it hard to spot the new ones, then it's time to switch apps or ditch the paper diary completely (or invest in a Tipp-Ex Mouse – a little roller where you don't have to wait for it to dry, it's a game-changer). If it's too time-consuming, then perhaps you're simply adding too much to your diary that could be relegated to to-do lists, or you're wasting time making a paper diary look pretty and it might be time to turn to the digital side.

An edited diary: top tips

Your calendar should make you feel organised to the point where you feel like you want to take a step back, take it all in and give yourself a pat on the back. Be proud of your diary! Sure, we can't always control what's being put into it, but we can control how we keep on top of it. Here are a few more tips to incorporate once you're a bit more familiar with your framework, to make your schedule do the hard work so you don't have to:

Add in birthdays and pop in a reminder a week before to send a card, and a gift if they're lucky. If you're using a digital calendar make sure it's set to recurring. I also add notes of things I've heard that person say that they'd love, which is why my mate Matt is getting a pasta maker this year.

The same goes for weddings and due dates. The minute I get a wedding invite I take a picture of it in case I misplace it, add the date to my diary with any extra notes regarding location, wedding lists and dress codes. Then for my mates' due dates I add those in my diary too. One, because it's nice to keep yourself a little free around that date to drop over a lasagne, and two, because it's handy for budgeting in for things like baby showers and expensive gifts from The White Company.

Work-wise, add in your deadlines – even if they're miles away – with a monthly countdown reminder if you feel that will put a rocket up your arse.

Write in the locations for meetings to save yourself desperately trying to find the original email as you elbow your way onto the bus. If you're going digital, make sure you send an invite to all attendees and add in notes or links that might come in handy during the meeting.

This tip only works if you're doing the digital route, but if you're not already, then operate two calendars. Keep one for personal appointments – like workouts, dentist/ doctor appointments and evening and weekend plans. Then have a work one for all your meetings, deadlines, project go-live dates and whatever else you need to keep tabs on. You can then always share your personal calendar with whoever you fancy, and your work calendar with colleagues – without your boss seeing that you've got a gynaecologist appointment tomorrow lunchtime.

If you're sticking with paper then whip out those highlighters and colour-code so it's easy to differentiate your personal tasks from your work ones, and your birthdays from your BodyPump classes.

We can be unrealistically optimistic when it comes to time, so make sure you have enough minutes between meetings to evaluate, catch up on missed tasks and head to the next. Meetings overrun and traffic is a royal pain in the arse, so always overestimate your timings and revel in your earliness at your next appointment.
LOOK AT YOU!

Unfortunately, diaries don't plan themselves, so try and get into a routine where you can plant yourself down for 20 minutes to plan, re-jig and use your diary to plan out your schedule for the week ahead. I find that a Friday evening or some time on a Sunday works best for me.
I know, a Friday evening? Such a party animal, me.

The Edit

Phew. One chapter down and I hope you're already feeling more organised than when you first picked up this book? Just a tad? I'll take that. Hopefully you've got your calendar *down*. You're checking it daily? You're updating it regularly? You're actually finding it a helpful tool in the planning and running of your everyday life – at work and at home? BRILLIANT. See, I told you, it seems like a minor detail but a well-planned diary makes everything else run like a well-oiled machine. Like Channing Tatum in *Magic Mike XXL*.

In terms of maintaining that scheduling muscle that you've worked so hard to build, just check in monthly to make sure your method is still working for you (no missed meetings, scheduling fails, forgotten appointments) and really work to nail down that weekly 20-minute planning session. It keeps you on top of things, plus gives you time to mentally take stock for the week ahead. Now you've warmed up on the organisation front, I think you're ready for the serious grown-up stuff. It's time to talk MONEY...

Money: the boring but crucial stuff

Budgeting is perhaps the least sexy part of an edited life but it is an important building block. So let's dial back the stress associated with money and get to grips with your own made-to-measure budget.

Financial planning is easily one of the most mundane aspects of #adulting. If you've yet to win on your lottery numbers, totting up your bank account figures isn't really the funnest of tasks. However, money can be one of the biggest stressors in our lives, and taking just 10 minutes on a weekly basis to evaluate our earnings and spending against a budget could mean the difference between sleeping like a baby, or a night spent tossing and turning and eventually ending up with a four-figure midnight-curated basket on ASOS that you 100% can't afford and therefore 100% want. Without a budget we can end up in a situation where we have no idea what's in (or not in) our accounts and where we lack the insight to pitch our finances against our life goals – whether that be saving for travel, a home, a baby or a handbag.

The idea of a budget might not be the easiest thing to stomach, but it's a juicy slice of the edited life pie…

Now that your diary is set up, financial planning sessions can be routinely added in. (DO IT: schedule them in like a meeting, to give them a sense of priority.)

Having a grip on your numbers will allow your soon-to-be-learnt self-care practices to tick over without your money worry stress levels strolling in to say hello every two seconds.

It will arm you with the base knowledge of your financial situation so you can plan ahead effectively, both in your home life and your career.

You'll know the figures in your bank account that can be spent on food, travel and at ASOS, and that will still allow you to pay your bills and save a little too.

A true breakdown of your spending might shock you at first, but once the initial 'OMG I spend *that* in Pret in a month!?' hysteria has calmed, you'll have the chance to prioritise your spending and slice up the pie however feels tastiest for you. Budgets have the stigma of being rigid, and that you'll be the pal always rejecting the offer of splitting the bill equally at dinner, but there's flexibility built in too. Inputs and outputs change and shift month to month, so a realistic budget needs to reflect that; having some general figures to aim for will assist you with planning and untie you from the weight of financial burdens that you've been dragging around for years.

During my time as a student and subsequent entry into the world of work, I buried my head in the sand and looked at my bank account fewer times a month than I could count on one hand. The part-time barmaid grind was monotonous, my income piddly and seeing a big fat minus in front of the total just wasn't a particularly thrilling experience. When it got to the point that I would breathe sigh of relief when a transaction was processed because I wasn't actually sure that there was enough in my account to buy yet ANOTHER peachy nude lipstick, I realised that things had to change – with my finances and my out-of-hand peachy nude lipstick habit.

It might have taken me a couple of years (and many 'how do you actually use a spreadsheet because I've forgotten what they taught me in school?' Google searches), but eventually a budget clicked into place for me. I eased myself in with the simple task of checking my bank account every couple of days. That alone was eye-opening. When you see the amount that gets eaten up IN A DAY by travel, a bite to eat for lunch, an off-the-cuff Amazon order and a mini food shop on the way home to pick up bits for dinner, it's enough to make you want to walk to work, pack your lunch, ditch the online shopping and do a weekly food shop right there. After two months of keeping close tabs on my spending, I felt I was ready to see it all laid out on the table, and got to creating myself a proper #adulting budget. I started with (and still continue to use) a Numbers spreadsheet and at first kept it simple by just tracking and observing what was coming out for all the boring stuff like bills and rent, what I was saving and how I spent what was left over. Eventually I split these sections down into a handful of categories, used my prior knowledge of my spending to create some numbers that would be ideal for me to aim for each month, threw in some visually pleasing colour-coding and that's still where I'm at all these years later. It took time to create and even more for it to sink in and become a monthly habit, but once it did I felt confident and in control of my financial situation for the first time ever. My overdraft was paid off in the blink of an eye, money for bills and rent was ready and waiting, and yes, I could afford that peachy nude lipstick, just not 10 of them.

Here's the mindset that I had to shift to: a budget isn't a punishment, it actually gives us an understanding of our finances that in turn gives us the knowledge and power to save and spend in a way that is most beneficial for us and our ambitions. Whipping out a spreadsheet isn't going to be for all of us, but at the very least aim to adopt these three mantras into your money habits:

DON'T LIVE BEYOND YOUR MEANS

Sounds obvious, but it can be harder to avoid than you think and it's the fast-track way to getting a big fat minus in front of your bank balance. Stick to the Prosecco now and you can pretend to like the Champagne later, because we all know Prosecco tastes better anyway.

LOOK AT YOUR BANK ACCOUNT AT LEAST TWICE A WEEK

To gain control over your finances, you have to know what's in there, even if it makes you throw up in your mouth a little bit. Download your bank's mobile app to make it even easier to keep updated. At least twice a week is the minimum that we should be taking a peek. Every day is optimal.

SAVE MONEY, LIKE, NOW

Even if it's £20 a month. Or a tenner. It creates a healthy habit and is something that you can slowly increase over time. 'Future You' will no doubt be making excuses for not saving yet, insisting that 'Even More in the Future You' will be the one to start. 'Present You' just has to suck it up and buy one less drink on a Friday.

How to set a budget

So by now you know you *need* to create yourself a budget, right? *insert collective groan*. Without a clear idea of what your incoming and outgoing figures are, your ability to plan ahead across all aspects of your life – travel, home, work, that new coat you check back on every day to make sure your size is still in stock – is hindered. In case you need more convincing, have a think of this. You know we're always being marketed to with this glossy, aspirational messaging and imagery of what our lives 'should' look like? Well, a budget can arm you with the knowledge of what is realistically possible given your current financial situation and therefore what is right for *you*. That teal velvet sofa might be something that you can save up for, but maybe the Scandi-inspired new-build apartment overlooking the city skyline just isn't in your scope right now. Screw the marketing! It's empowering stuff even if it makes you want to yawn.

It's impossible to cover everything there is to know about budgets in just one chapter of a book. The available resources out there on the topic are seriously vast and I'll add some of the ones that I've found most helpful over the years in the **Resources** section, along with links to PDF documents that are up on my blog theannaedit.com if you're more a print-out worksheet whizz. This is more of a 'dip your toe in' taster, and I'd highly recommend that, once you've worked your way through the stages that I've proposed here, you deep-dive into further literature, especially if it's a step that you enjoyed getting stuck into. Once you find the method that works for you, the resulting feeling of financial confidence is a rewarding and badass one.

This section is meaty so take your time with it. If you're just not ready to take it on right now, then scan over it and bookmark the chapter to tackle later. Even if you do decide to dig in, the process of implementing a budget takes months, so you'll probably find yourself having to revisit these pages. Basically you're about to become *very* familiar with the upcoming text. If you're already au fait with a budget then skip to the end where I share my top tips for year-round saving and making seasonal cuts. In terms of budgeting, though, there are five stages to working your way up to a fully functioning one, so let's get to it.

STEP 1: CHECK YOUR ACCOUNT

If your heart is already racing at the thought of checking your current
account balance, then ease yourself in by trying to incorporate the
'once a day' rule. Set a recurring alarm on your phone at a suitable time
each day for you to have this heart-pounding moment (I promise your
bpm decreases over time) when you open up your banking app and
assess your transactions from the past 24 hours. Although you might be
chomping at the bit to get stuck in with a cold, hard budget, this initial
tracking period is an important one because it forces you to get familiar
with your money flows and to spot the various streams in which you're
spending your cash. I'd recommend sticking with this step for a period
of two weeks, or up to a month, depending on how confident you feel
with your bank account already. Over time, curiosity will set up shop,
and the need to know more, save more and get stuck in with the maths
will creep in (*hopefully*).

STEP 2: WHAT'S GOING IN AND GOING OUT?

So you've been checking your account daily like a pro for at least
two weeks and you're ready for the next step? Before creating a
spreadsheet that you need a master's degree to operate, let's create
something simpler that is user-friendly to navigate, and to input
and pull out all the relevant numbers from. This step is a mixture
of tracking, like you've already been doing – using a budgeting
framework but in its very simplest form.

There are four figures to think about when it comes to setting a
budget: your **net monthly or weekly income** (that's your income after
all taxes and deductions have been made), your **fixed expenses** that
stay the same every month (like your rent or mortgage, bills, transport),
your **variable expenses** that fluctuate from month to month (like
food shopping, eating out, entertainment, shopping) and then what
you should be **saving** or **repaying** (either in ISAs, savings accounts or
paying off debts such as student or other loans, outstanding credit card
bills or overdrafts).

1. Set yourself up a spreadsheet (either Excel or Numbers will do) and add the months of the year across the top row, and your categories – **net income**, **fixed expenses**, **variable expenses** and **savings & debts** – vertically down a left-hand column. I suggest using your spending from the previous month as your starting point.

	JANUARY	FEBRUARY	MARCH
Net income			
Fixed expenses			
Variable expenses			
Savings & debts			

2. Input your net income in the relevant box.

	JANUARY	FEBRUARY	MARCH
Net income	£1,800		
Fixed expenses			
Variable expenses			
Savings & debts			

3. Print out your statement from the previous month and categorise each transaction by highlighting in a colour that identifies it with the relevant expense – either **fixed**, **variable** or **savings & debts**. Here's a snapshot from my account:

RATE	ACCOUNT	AMOUNT	CATEGORY
30.01	ISA account	£250	**savings & debts**
30.01	HelloFresh	£34.99	**variable expense**
01.02	iTunes	£6.99	**variable expense**
01.02	Joint account (money for mortgage and bills)	£750	**fixed expense**

4   Once you've categorised every transaction you've made that past month, add all the figures from each category together until you have a total number for each of the three expense headings. Input those figures into the relevant box in your spreadsheet, and there in a snapshot you'll be able to see how your income is being split each month; how much is going on **fixed expenses**, the money that's going towards your **variable expenses** and what you've managed to **save** each month and/or put towards paying off your debts.

	JANUARY	FEBRUARY	MARCH
Net income	£1,800		
Fixed expenses	£850		
Variable expenses	£625		
Savings & debts	£250		

5   Once you've inputted the previous month's figures, update your figures in your current month's column weekly if possible to avoid a mass printing situation, as it will be easier to quickly scan over your account off your desktop or app and input numbers, just adding to them every week and totting them up ready for analysis at the end of the month. Do this step for two to three months, which will not only get you in the swing of having a weekly finance session, but also a chance to notice any patterns of spending that emerge.

STEP 3: ANALYSE

Well, firstly, soak it in. Does the split look like how you were imagining it? Or is your **variable expenses** spend making your eyeballs pop out of your head? What you do with your findings is going to depend on what your financial goals are. I'd avoid doing anything too drastic while you're still trying out this step, as you're not really seeing the detail here, more a brief overview (so step away from Net-a-Porter immediately). Instead assess how it makes you feel, and use this time to really try to pin down what you'd like to achieve out of your budget. Have a mull over these scenarios. If you feel like you're spending too much on your **fixed expenses** then it's worth looking into switching gas or electricity suppliers to see if you can decrease your bills, or maybe scouting out cheaper accommodation. If it's your **variable expenses** that are taking the largest split then it might be time to ease on dining out or pull back your lunchtime Zara hauls a tad. Typically, for most of us it's going to be our lack of **savings** that isn't a shocking discovery, but is where it takes a bit of balancing to see where we can scrimp and save in the other categories in order to compensate. Here's where the next step comes in.

STEP 4: THE 50:30:20 SPLIT

You no longer feel like you might keel over when you have to check your bank account and you actually have an understanding of what your cash flow is looking like, plus you've familiarised yourself with spreadsheets for the first time in 12 years. I mean, you might as well just apply for your Chartership in Accounting right this second. Now it's time to turn this tracking budget into an actual budget and plug in some numbers to aim for. There's no one set budget format that's going to work for all, so it's worth taking the example here, plugging in your figures and seeing where it needs editing.

The general consensus is that your **net income** should split three ways, divided up something like this: 50% for your **fixed expenses**, 30% for your **variable expenses** and 20% for **savings & debts**.

The first step is to evaluate your spreadsheet so far. The tracking that you've inputted already is useful information that will help you to tweak and curate your ideal budget. We're not starting from scratch here – PROMISE. Heck, you've put in three months of groundwork by this point. Let's see how your previous spending fits in with the 50:30:20 ideal budget. Highlight your fixed expenses, variable expenses and savings & debts for one month, select the chart function and then the pie chart option and there you have a breakdown of how your budget pie slices up so far. Do this for every month that you've tracked so far – do you notice any patterns? Are they all similar? Is one month completely different to the others? Is your savings slice way off the 20% marker?

CHART 1

5%

25%

70%

CHART 2

10%

30%

60%

Fixed expenses   Variable expenses   Savings & debts

CHART 1 In this example, fixed expenses are eating up most of the income. Perhaps rent is particularly high and could be decreased by downsizing a little, or moving to a more affordable part of town? Savings are particularly low, but hey, 5% is better than 0%.

CHART 2 Here it's variable expenses that are taking up a large proportion of the budget. Actually, this is quite a healthy problem to have as it means that there is room in your income to put a much larger proportion into savings, if you can cut down the extra spending.

While tracking your headline figures is conducive to seeing an overall breakdown, it's not that useful in helping us to unearth exactly why those figures look like they do. Here's where I'd recommend expanding your spreadsheet further. Under the **fixed expenses** box, add in a handful more rows and fill those cells with categories to break down your spending into. So for **fixed expenses** that could be your rent/mortgage payment, utilities (water, electric, gas), travel expenses and phone bill, for example.

	APRIL	MAY	JUNE
Net income	£1,800		
Fixed expenses	£850		
Rent	£650		
Utilities	£100		
Transport	£40		
Phone bill	£60		
Variable expenses	£625		
Savings & debts	£250		

It's a lengthy process when you're inputting your data into your budget to categorise your spending in this way, as there are more categories to collate and therefore more sums to do. However, it arms us with a magnifying glass to snoop into our spending and habits, and with that level of understanding, we can *finally* work out what our ideal budget looks like.

Repeat this step for **variable expenses** and **savings & debts** too. Do the same as you did in the previous stage, by printing off your statement, grouping the transactions into categories by highlighting them in different colours and then totting up the figures and adding the sum into the relevant sub-category. Here are the sub-categories that I suggest using:

FIXED EXPENSES	VARIABLE EXPENSES	SAVINGS & DEBTS
Rent/mortgage payments	Food shopping	General savings (direct debits, ISAs etc.)
Utilities (water, electric, gas)	Entertainment (eating out, cinema, bars etc.)	Loan repayments (student or personal)
Car expenses	Health (gym fees, class costs, dentist, prescriptions)	Pension contributions
Public transport		
Household expenditures (council tax, maintenance fees, insurances etc)	Gifts and donations	Savings for a particular event (travel, wedding, moving etc.)
Phone and internet bills	Subscriptions (magazines, book clubs, online viewing platforms)	
Childcare	Personal care (toiletries, hair-cuts, waxes etc)	
	Shopping	

The important thing to remember is that, as with all best-laid plans, there needs to be some flexibility. With the current rocketing costs of city-living, there's going to be a fair amount of you who are going to be nowhere near the 50:30:20 split because your accommodation costs are going to skew it in the **fixed expenses** direction. Incomes change, some months are packed with birthdays (I see you, all you September-born, Christmas-conceived friends!), others are so cold that you can't be arsed to leave the house. So know that you won't hit the mark perfectly every time, but if you're sticking close to the parameters and you have a general understanding of where your money *should* be going and where it actually *is* going, that is a good place to be. Spend two months inputting your spending into your newly detailed spreadsheet, checking it weekly to see how it breaks down into the 50:30:20 suggested pie chart and noting the results. Then it's time to edit…

STEP 5: EDIT IT TO FIT YOU
(THE REST OF YOUR LIFE! LOL!)

So your budget looks a little beefier now, right? You can see if your costs for eating out are more than they are for eating in. Or if you overdosed on retail therapy? Took more Ubers than you wish to admit? Realised that your phone bill is one of your biggest money drains? When it's all out on the table like this – quite literally – there's nowhere for the figures to hide, and with your detailed breakdown there for you to take in it should be clear to see what categories need to be pulled back a little in order to up the figures elsewhere.

By this point you'll have two months of broken down sub-categorised spreadsheet inputting under your belt. So now I'd recommend running your spending from the previous two months into a pie chart again – focusing on the total figures for **fixed expenses**, **variable expenses** and **savings & debts** categories. Firstly, does the chart come close to the 50:30:20 split? Secondly, how does it compare with your charts from the previous months? Are you consistent with your spending in each category? If not, why not? Was it travel that knocked you off? A friend's wedding and hen do, and subsequent gift? Make a note of that and factor that in next time you have a holiday booked or a mate gets hitched. This is the point to digest all the information that you've soaked up over the previous six months, and to turn it into something truly beautiful that is going to give you more financial control that you ever had before.

Create yourself a new column: this is going to be your experimenting area where you can play around with figures in each category, make a pie chart to see what the split is like, tweak some more and have a think about whether your proposed budget is going to work with the life you currently have and the life you want (I know, SO DEEP). If you need somewhere to start then use the figures that match up to the 50:30:20 split. Do you think you could work to that framework, or is that just not right for you currently? It's a process and might cut a whole afternoon from your schedule, but attempt to settle on a clear figure that you wish to spend next month on each category, while being realistic. FINALLY – A BUDGET!

	JULY	AUGUST (PROPOSED)	AUGUST
Net income	£1,800	£1,800	
Fixed expenses	£850	£900	
Rent	£650	£650	
Utilities	£100	£100	
Transport	£80	£90	
Phone bill	£80	£60	
Variable expenses	£625	£540	
Food	£300	£240	
Entertainment	£125	£100	
Exercise classes	£70	£70	
Subscriptions	£30	£30	
Shopping	£100	£100	
Savings & debts	£250	£360	
ISA contributions	£250	£250	
Holiday savings	£0	£50	
Total remaining:	**£75**	**£60**	

So in this proposed budget, the transport spend is increased slightly so you could get the bus every day – as it's summer and it's just too hot to walk – but actually that brings the **fixed expenses** up to a 50% split which is a-ok. The **variable expenses** have been decreased by reducing the spend for food (easily done with some meal planning and batch-cooking) and there's been a small reduction in the entertainment category, but this has increased the **savings** amount so that you could begin to put money away for a weekend city-break you have coming up. I've also added in a total remaining row as it's always good to have some residual cash left over just in case. This could be added into **savings & debts** the following month.

If you're struggling to see how your spending can be malleable, especially with **fixed expenses**, just remember that you're in control of at least 90% of your outgoings. If your rent is too high, then it might be time to move. If you're eating out too much *raises hand*, then factor in more home-cooked meals. If the slice of your savings pie is a lowly 5% then look at where you can claw back in the other two categories to oomph it up. Or perhaps 5% is all you can afford right now, and – let's face it – it's better than zero. It's going to be different for everyone, so don't be afraid to tweak it. Finding the right budget balance is a constant editing process. One month might come in under budget by a mile and the next might swing completely the opposite way. If your ideal budget row isn't working for you, then swap out the figures for new ones. The longer you track for, the more familiar you'll become with your ideal figures; knowing that you might have £50 in your budget for personal care each month means that you know for a fact that you should book in your next bikini wax in eight weeks' time instead of four. It gives a structure and mindfulness to your spending. We're not aiming for Monica-like perfection here, just to be at a place where you feel like you are in charge of your finances and they're not being the boss of you.

My current budget

Here's what my current budget looks like and how I'm trying to better balance the scales in my spending:

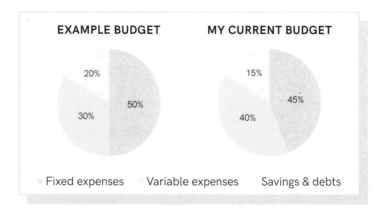

EXAMPLE BUDGET

20%
30%
50%

MY CURRENT BUDGET

15%
40%
45%

Fixed expenses   Variable expenses   Savings & debts

- FIXED EXPENSES We've managed to get our bills down by switching energy providers, going for SIM-only contracts on our mobiles and shunning the money-pit upgrades.

- VARIABLE EXPENSES This is where I need to cut back. Too many takeaways. Too much eating out. Too many Gucci loafers (but seriously, what a GREAT investment – but we'll get to that).

- SAVINGS Again, this is a slice that I need to increase and where I need to practise what I preach – present Anna, suck it up! I've since set up a direct debit so money goes into my savings each month without me being able to peck away at it till it gets down to zero.

Let's get down to business

I thought I'd just give a quick shout-out to my fellow self-employed crew, because I've learnt a few things during my seven years of working for myself – aside from all-day snacking being a great perk. Firstly: get yourself an accountant. A really good one, who replies to you promptly, is happy to talk you through all the money mumbo jumbo and is someone you trust to advise you on all financial business matters. If you're looking for recommendations, ask friends or those who work in a similar field for their suggestions. If you're struggling for positive testimonials then comb the Internet for reviews (unbiased. co.uk offers a search engine for Chartered Accountants), although I think it's preferable to have an in-person endorsement, and so you should exhaust all avenues that could lead to that first. If you're early on in the game and can't afford an accountant, then look into online accounting software like xero.com, which is still an expense, but makes the bookkeeping process super-easy to track and follow. Secondly: always file and pay your taxes on time. The fines just ain't worth it, and is precious money that could be going on snacks.

Whether you're self-employed or not, and it sounds like I'm wagging my finger at you as I write this, it's worth thinking about the future. You might not be considering buying a home now, but you may be in a few years, so ask your accountant how best to set up your business and books should you want to get on the property ladder at a later date. Have the conversation about pensions, too, while you're at it. Got to make sure you have some pennies saved for all your garden centre visits! Ha. Who am I kidding? I go to garden centres *now* on a monthly basis.

MY BUDGETING TOP TIPS

- Buy a calculator. I know that sounds like an order from the Dark Ages, but I made an Amazon order for one approximately two minutes after I started my first ever budget. I use the banking app on my phone to find the figures, pump them into my calculator and then input them into Numbers on my laptop. Yes, your laptop could do it all, but I find that having all three interfaces open in front of me is the quickest way to get it done.

- Although it's tempting to break down your spending into 50+ different categories so you can see every minute detail of what you're spending your money on, I'd suggest that to begin with you stick to five to seven categories max for each of the three slices. It makes the whole thing less confusing, and if you do fancy seeing an itemised breakdown of your expenditure, that's what your bank statement is for.

- The tracking process can be really time-consuming at first: book it into your calendar like an official meeting so you treat it with priority, and fit it in weekly if you can. Leaving it till the end of the month, when typically work becomes busy with deadlines and our social lives pick up a bit more because everyone has been paid, isn't the smartest idea.

- Remember to be flexible. After all, a budget is simply a guideline. Think of it as a helping hand from your super-frugal mate who hasn't spent more than a tenner on anything in the past 10 years and you're convinced must be a secret millionaire by now. If anything, it's a great indicator of whether an aspect of your life needs shaking up; whether it's indicating that you need to move, ask for a promotion, look for a new job that doesn't require such a pricey commute, or you need to address why you and your DPD delivery driver are best mates.

A quick note on 'Treat Yo' Self' purchases. We all fancy something nice or need the odd pick-me-up from time to time, and although J.Lo said her *'love don't cost a thing'*, sometimes nice treats do. If it's a REALLY expensive bag or dress or holiday that you're after, I'd recommend saving for it and using a row from the **savings & debts** column to create your own special fund for that particular purchase. In terms of buying things in general, often we *need* to update our clothing because it's worn out, or sometimes we *need* something for our home. Other times we just *want* to buy a top from Cos on our lunch break for no other reason than because we feel we deserve a 'Treat Yo' Self' moment. To tackle this in the budget, I'd suggest having a row under the **variable expenses** category for necessary purchases like replacing worn items or general bits and bobs that you can't really go without. Then have a row for non-essential shopping purchases, aka *the wants*. Even if you just stick £20 in there it gives you the feeling that you can buy a lipstick on the way home if you want to, and if by the end of the month it's not been used, stick it in your savings.

The category that we're all likely to struggle with and overspend on is undoubtedly **variable expenses**. I mean, the clue is in the name. It's not consistent! I'd recommend an app to help you with this. Monzo is a pre-paid card that categorises all your variable spending into easily digested analytics that you can access on your mobile. Not only does this make adding the figures into your budget quicker, it can give you an on-the-spot view of your spending. My husband Mark transfers all his **variable expenses** budget over onto the card when he gets paid and uses it for all purchases throughout the month. Genius.

Easy ways to save money, now

How many times have you scanned a magazine, blog or your Twitter feed and spotted an article titled 'Easy Ways to Save Money NOW!'? I'm guessing it's easily a double-digit number. Now think how many times you've read that article, absorbed it, actually taken the advice and put it into practice? I'm guessing the figure is far less impressive. Why do we play ourselves like that? Of course there are going to be some exceptions to the rule, but for the majority of us who are ignoring the recommendations or just can't be arsed to apply them, the fact of the matter is that with just a few not particularly groundbreaking shifts and tweaks here and there, we could be saving ourselves possibly hundreds of pounds a year. That's the spa day you think you can't afford/your car insurance that you were struggling to scrape together/a fancy meal out with your family, right there on a platter.

So let's start this one off on the right foot this time. Sure, the suggestions that are realistically applicable are going to be different for everyone, but as a budget-busting baseline, why not give *one* of them a go immediately. From this point on make one of the following your own money mantra. You'll soon start to see the pounds stacking up, and before you know it you'll be the bore who lectures their mates on the benefits of loyalty cards on a Friday night down the pub.

CUT THE COFFEE

It's a classic one, but skipping your coffee on the way to work could be saving you in excess of £10 a week, which equates to £520 a year. THAT'S CRAZY. Either make it at home and sip from your flask at your desk, keep a set of your own coffee-making supplies at the office, or if you just can't shake your morning stop-at-the-coffee-shop habit, invest in a reusable keep cup that not only saves you up to 50p per coffee, but also means you're doing your bit for the environment too.

FORGET ABOUT THE CLUB

Ditch the memberships that you never use. The obvious one to point out here is gym membership. For those of us who can't even remember what a hip abductor machine looks like, make cancelling your membership top of your to-do list. Either pocket the savings, or spend the money going to a class that you actually enjoy (if you like them, buy the sessions in bulk as it usually ends up cheaper). Have a think too about other memberships or subscription services that you're no longer getting the use out of. Is your magazine subscription still sitting in the plastic wrap two months later? CANCEL. Is your fresh food box humming in the corner because you didn't get round to cooking it before it went mouldy? CANCEL. Look over the back end of your iTunes account to see if you have any active app subscriptions that you could cancel, and check your bank account for direct debits to services you wouldn't miss if you waved goodbye to them.

LEARN TO LOVE LISTS

We'll cover this in greater detail later on down the edited life road, but never shop without a list, whether it's for food, gifts or clothing. If you see something you like that you didn't originally set out for, leave it at least two days before you purchase it. Take a time out. Mull it over and consult your budget. There's a high possibility of you talking yourself out of it once the impulse has passed.

DITCH THE UPGRADE

Once you've broken down your spending and formed a budget, there's a high chance that one of your priciest bills aside from accommodation and food is your phone bill. So instead of opting in for an upgrade next time it comes around, keep your old phone and switch to a SIM-only deal, which usually ends up being half the price of your old contract. No one cares that your phone is five years old. Is it an iPhone 10? 20? I have no idea, and I know I sound like your grandma but if it does everything that you need it to do, and it's performing its functions well enough, then it's worth keeping for now. Plus, that's more money back into your budget that could be distributed elsewhere.

SKIP THE PRIME-TIME VIEWING

Do you only ever watch Netflix? More of an Amazon Prime Instant Video kinda person? Ditch your cable package and if you never watch TV either, sell it and save yourself the licence fee, too (side note: I do realise this is a bit extreme and I could personally never go without my *Great British Bake Off* viewing, but it's a good tip for students who are looking to scrape back some serious pennies).

GET SALES SAVVY

Sales shopping is a tricky one. On the one hand you can secure yourself a huge saving on a big-ticket item that you've had your eye on for months. On the other it can be the epitome of impulse shopping, where you spend a small fortune and end up with a sequin top that looked great in the changing room, but in the cold light of day doesn't seem like the best move, and a footstool that you can't actually fit in your front room but was a third off. Here's the thing, though: 50% off is still 50% on. You're still spending money, even though it might be less than the RRP. I'd recommend arming yourself with a strict list before you leave for battle. Have a good think about gaps in your wardrobe and home that need filling, confer with your budget the amount you'd like to spend and STICK TO IT. Keep your blinkers on and your receipts in a safe place, so if you get home and realise you've made a big mistake, don't be put off by how hell-like the customer service will be: suck it up and get your refund ASAP.

BE A LOYAL CUSTOMER

Sign up for loyalty cards at the stores you shop in regularly. Some are pants but others can earn you decent savings on your food, fuel, travel and toiletries. I'd recommend signing up to your supermarket and petrol station of choice, all airline loyalty schemes that you travel on and getting yourself a Boots Advantage Card. It might take you seven years, but that bottle of perfume that you like can be yours FOR FREE if you buy every single toiletry product you ever need from Boots.

Seasonal savings

Year-round saving hacks are great, but some months of the year are going to be financially tighter than others. So when you're feeling the pinch, it's good to have seasonal suggestions to deploy that are able to claw back the spending and put the balance back into your ingoing/outgoing figures during the months you need it the most.

SPRING

- Sift through any gift vouchers you received over the holidays and mark the dates down in your diary when each expires. That way you're not missing out on any potential purchases, and the gift giver won't end up offended as the voucher gathers dust.

- Spring tends to be an off-peak season for most holiday destinations within easy reach of the UK, so although you're not exactly *saving* money in the traditional sense here, if you do want a cheap break then snap up a holiday during the springtime.

Make money while you spring clean by posting your unwanted clothing and accessories for sale online. Depop or Facebook Marketplace are great places to list high-street goods, then save your really fancy stuff for Vestiaire Collective, a designer pre-loved website that authenticates your item for your buyer for a cut of the price.

If you're sticking to holidaying in the summer season, look into getting cashback on your vacation-related purchases by using sites like topcashback.co.uk, where a percentage of each transaction (think accommodation, flights, travel insurance) goes directly back into your bank account.

Everything for your holiday booked? Bag packed and ready to go? Make sure you've budgeted for your trip, too: work out how much currency you want to change up before you end up at the airport and pluck a number out of thin air.

Make the most of the five days a year that it's warm enough to do outdoor activities and skimp on your entertainment budget by enjoying some sausages cooked up on a BBQ in your back garden, a picnic in the park or a walk in the countryside with a packed lunch.

If your home is a little chilly, spend this season winter-proofing it before the cold front makes an appearance. Budget in for roofers to insulate your loft, get a quote to refurbish your windows if they are past their best, buy blackout curtains for an extra thermal layer and fit draught excluders to your doors.

October is quite the month for health-related initiatives that will not only help you clean up your internal act, but will also stop you spending a healthy slice of your **variable expenses**. Stoptober is an annual nationwide NHS campaign encouraging people to quit smoking, and Go Sober For October does what it says on the tin. If you're looking to cut back in either (or both!) of these areas, autumn is the time to hop on board.

- It's a classic, but budget in for all your Christmas spending now and spread the cost over the next four months instead of just the one. I'm not only talking about presents here; factor in any Christmas parties, food, booze, outfits you might want to buy, decorations, winter weddings and your New Year's Eve plans too.

- Get on the Christmas card train early with the incentive of planning ahead and saving money by using a batch of second-class stamps. It might seem like a piddly change, but first class stamps are pricey; if you've got a list as long as your arm to send out… GET ON IT.

- Homemade baked gifts go down a treat if you're looking for a way to cut back your present-buying budget, such as a gigantic jar of mincemeat, festive-shaped gingerbreads or a box of homemade chocolate mints. I always make a few extra to have on hand for when unexpected gifts are handed over.

- If your family circle is rather large or you're all just trying to keep your Christmas costs down, implement a Secret Santa system. You all pick a name out of a hat, set a budget and buy a gift for just that one person. There are only five of us in our family, but it helps to take the stress out of shopping and usually ends up making us all cry with laughter as we try and guess who has who.

Some seasons will be spendier than others, but by preparing yourself for these shifts in cashflow throughout the year you should be able to keep your books running smoothly, whatever the weather and whatever Hallmark holiday is on the horizon.

The Edit

Budgeting is a meaty subject in the grand scheme of an edited life, and so it isn't one that I wanted to brush over. I hope I've achieved my aim of giving you a base-level understanding of all things money, so that the next time you look at your bank balance you know how to tackle it without the side order of heart palpitations. If you have decided to go full steam ahead with a budget then be patient (and insert party popper emoji here). Other ideas in this book can be applied immediately with instant results, but budgeting is a slow burner, and the longer you stew over it, the more likely your confidence in your cashflow management skills will hit that tasty sweet spot.

Budgeting is essentially a balancing act, and it's tough to hit the nail on the head of perfection 100% of the time. If you slip up, THAT'S COOL. You might go for the mobile upgrade or buy a ridiculous coat that can't be dry cleaned and that tips you over your clothing spend for the month (not that I'm speaking from experience with that one *at all*), but the important thing to remember is that just because you might have frittered your money away one day by pretending you were Mariah Carey in a music video, waving all your paper around, the next day doesn't have to be a repeat. Dust yourself off, consult on just how much damage was done, work out how you can reach an equilibrium-*ish* again, and move on. Hopefully you know how to track and how to budget using the methods I've outlined here – but edited by yourself, for yourself. Speaking of which, now it's time to focus on you...

Self-care

The clue is in the name here: in order to operate in our most efficient and content way we must take care of ourselves, so use this chapter to focus on you, your mental health and your wellbeing habits and routines.

Although the term 'self-care' can seem like an industry-invented idea instigated in order to push sales of luxury bath salts and cashmere socks, I'm here to tell you to believe the hype (and that cashmere socks will be one of the most eye-rolling yet best buys you will ever make). In the realm of an edited life, self-care is defined by all and any routines, behaviours and habits that allow you to push yourself a notch higher on the wellbeing scale. This might even include being on top of your budget and your diary, as they can allow you space for less anxiety and more sleep, but more often than not it's a moment for yourself that allows you to press pause on whatever else is going on, to block out the noise and get your inner battery levels up. Self-care is not only an important skill to master in terms of your health, happiness and overall wellbeing, it's also fundamental to clearing out the mental clutter, and will aid you in becoming more efficient, motivated and productive. So it's time to get on the hype train.

Here's the important thing to get your head around: there's a stereotype that self-care is the ultimate luxury, only to be devoured by the rich and famous, who slope around in fluffy robes having poo-sucking tubes stuck up their bums and a plethora of vom-inducing herbal teas served to them in bone china. However, a mum-of-two's definition of self-care might be locking herself in the loo for two minutes and flicking through the latest gossip rag in order to get just 120 seconds of peace. Or maybe you start work at the crack of dawn when a visit to the gym just isn't feasible, so you do a session of at-home yoga in front of the TV when you finish your shift instead. Being on your own might be the definition of self-care for some, or personal hell for others, when an evening out with friends will allow you to plug your battery pack back in. The underlying factor is that self-care enables you a chunk of time – no matter how long or short – to do something for yourself that recharges your energy reserves in whatever way you find works best. That's the only goal.

The four pillars of self-care

In order to truly care for ourselves we need to go a step further than just running a bath once a week and turning ourselves into prunes while we worry about that niggling problem at work. In fact, I believe that there are four pillars to focus on:

MENTAL HEALTH

SLEEP

EATING WELL

PHYSICAL ACTIVITY

I've put mental health first on the list because it's the most important aspect of self-care, HANDS DOWN. Let's listen to ourselves more, be kinder, give ourselves a rest and assess how and why we're feeling the way we are. We all feel better when we've had a good night's sleep, *fact*. So that one goes without saying. Eating well can be a pain in the balls when all you fancy chowing down on is a McDonald's Bacon & Egg McMuffin, but fuelling ourselves with fresh and wholesome food will work in unison with all the other pillars to have you feeling in tip-top condition. Think Sasha Fierce mode. Finally, I'm throwing physical activity into the ring, because it clears the mind, aids sleep and will help you work up an appetite. You see? It's all one big ol' self-care wheel where each feeds into the other, and by working on even just one of the moving parts, the others are all going to have a positive knock-on effect too.

When it comes to self-care and integrating it into our lives, routines are GOLDEN. In fact they're what we're aiming for here. Keeping a cap on our stress levels becomes easier once we're able to slip into a routine that we know works to quieten the noise. Dreamworld is knocking at the door once we've devised a bedtime routine that makes our eyelids feel heavy. Eating well is a doddle when we get our head around planning a weekly food shop and meal-prep routine. So it's no surprise that working out slowly becomes ingrained in our lives in a way that's hard to remove once we create a routine around it.

Realistically, it's a fair amount to take in, and with life being a constant editing process, we're not likely to feel like we're completely acing each pillar all of the time – and that's completely ok. In fact even if we're just taking a quick moment before we sleep to think about the highs and lows of the day, going to bed just 20 minutes earlier than we were before, meal-prepping our breakfasts to streamline our morning routine and getting off the bus to work one stop early to get some extra steps logged into our day, that's more than enough, and isn't that great? I'd place a bet that just by incorporating those small self-care changes that don't even eat into that much time, you'll be feeling that you have your shit just a little bit more together.

You don't need to book whole days out of your schedule (or maybe you do if you've reached burnout, and that's something medical professionals can help with), nor does it need to chip away into your budget, but it is about making an investment in yourself. You're probably ticking plenty of these self-care items off the list anyway without even realising it, and taking the time to relish them. You take the dog for a walk and listen to a podcast while you do it? FAB. You make sure you have some greens with your dinner? BRILLIANT. You slope off during your lunch to read a book in the break room. GO YOU – WHAT YOU READING? Self-care doesn't need to be about grand gestures, it's just about making these small tweaks that will all ultimately add up to make you feel bloomin' great in your day-to-day life.

Mental health

Mental health – let's have a chat about it. The Survey of Mental Health and Wellbeing, published in 2016 by NHS Digital, showed that around one in six adults in England met the criteria for a common mental health disorder. On the bright side, attitudes to mental health are constantly shifting towards a place where the stigma is removed, open and honest conversations are welcomed, and help is there when needed.

Sometimes we have a shit week where we can't seem to focus and all we want to do is have a bath and read a book in bed in the foetal position. Then Friday rolls around and you get the chance to run yourself some bubbles and flick through the pages of your latest read and all is ok in the world again. Other times a shit week becomes a shit month, which becomes a shit year and the fog is so heavy that no amount of baths or early nights in bed with a book are going to solve it. In those instances all I can suggest is talking. Talk to a friend, a family member, someone at work, a professional, your GP; whoever feels comfortable and right. It's important to understand that sometimes lighting a candle and slipping into silky soft pyjamas just isn't enough. These simple acts of self-care and life editing may combine to take the edge off the darkness a little, but often professional advice and subsequent assistance are the best course of action to fully pull yourself out. Sending lots of love and a big ol' hug your way.

While we're on the topic of 'crap things that aren't particularly fun, but are important to talk about', let's chat about stress. Ah yes, that old chestnut. Unfortunately, it's something that we encounter often, whether it's a feeling that we're experiencing ourselves, or our BFFs telling us on the phone that they're just too stressed to function. It might sound like a millennial moan, but it needs to be taken seriously, and it's helpful to learn how to manage it in order to prevent it from becoming detrimental to our daily lives or causing physical harm. Let's try and keep those hearts healthy, eh? It's often experienced when we feel like we're under too much mental and emotional pressure, and it's something that every individual handles in a unique way. What could cause one person to have a sob down the phone to their other half might be a complete walk in the park for others. Through applying these self-care practices to your life, when things get noisy you'll be able to twist the volume down to just the right level by spotting your own triggers and thresholds, and editing your routine in the appropriate way to keep stress at bay.

As there's no 'one-size-fits-all' approach with stress, I'd be wasting my words typing out advice on the trillion different things you could try to tackle it (and that sounds stressful in itself!). So I'd recommend these steps the next time you feel the s-word swelling up inside:

1   Take a short pause to work out the reasons why you're feeling like you want to bury your head in the sand (whether there are two items on your list or 200).

2. Read back through them. Are they worries that are out of your control and therefore something you just have to let go? If so, cross them out. They're mental clutter that needs to be shown the door. Or are they things that you have the power to change? Fab. Highlight them.

3. Work to formulate an action plan for each point, based on past techniques that have worked for you, or new ones that you wish to give a go that might crush it, or at least dial those emotions back to a level that feels manageable.

4. Feeling better already? Brilliant. Either crack on with your plans, adding any to-dos to your schedule, dates to your diary and getting on task, or sit back and relax if you feel the stress has melted away and exited your brain for now.

I'm a classic 'too much on my plate' stress-er, so whenever I look in my diary and see a sea of appointments, deadlines and meetings, I FREAK OUT. So helpful, I know, for someone who has a fair amount of appointments, deadlines and meetings. In these instances, after following the steps above I attempt to take it back to feeling chill AF as the kids like to say these days, with the following methods. Be warned, all the clichéd classics work best for me, so while these might not be exactly groundbreaking, they do the trick...

MY FIVE FAVOURITE STRESS RELIEVERS

A GOOD BOOK

It wasn't until last year that I really dug back into my bookshelf and picked up reading as a hobby again, just like my pre-teen *Sweet Valley High*-obsessed self did back at the turn of the millennium. Of course, being the annoying teacher's pet that I am, it began as a New Year's Resolution that I solidified in the form of a 12-book challenge for 2018 (side note: the Goodreads app is a great way to track this). In the end I sunk down almost double that figure. Not only has it created an evening routine that helps me to nod off, it also provides an escape that allows me to completely switch off; an activity to lose myself in when all I would be doing instead is scrolling aimlessly on my phone until

I found something worthy of sending to the 'CUTE GIF' WhatsApp group I have with my friends. It also focuses my brain on a long-form task, in a world of 240-character tweets and snappy five-minute-read articles, which is something that it doesn't engage in enough. Glazing over in front of the TV doesn't have the same effect as making sense of written material, and often my before-bed reads can be the only time in my day when I'm fully centred in that way for a long period of time.

AN EVENING AT-HOME SPA

OH HELLO OBVIOUS INCLUSION! But seriously, who doesn't love pretending that their bathroom is a spa (except one that plays *Queer Eye* on your laptop, instead of blasting out whale music)? For me there's nothing quite like it. I limit myself to 'spa-time' once a week because, you know, we have to save water/save the planet and all that. However, during those times I go *all out*. I file my feet, shave my legs, put on a hair mask and wash it out so I feel like I'm in an anti-dandruff hair-swishing advert, moisturise all over, bathe my cuticles in oil, do a face mask and finish it off with the pièce de résistance – fresh pyjamas. I understand that this sounds like a lengthy process, but that's kind of the point. As the Fab Five preach, taking a time out to indulge in self-maintenance can not only help to ease anxiety, but also bolster your self-confidence. I know I feel pants if my hair is looking like you could fry an egg on it and my nail polish is only covering a third of my nail. Book yourself in, stay for as long as you can and soak the stress away.

At-home spa essentials:
- Bath Salts/Oils
- Foot File/Body Exfoliator
- Body Oil
- Hair Mask
- Face Mask
- Facial Oil/Treatment

A FEAST

This isn't going to be such a universally appreciated inclusion, I know, as for some people cooking is a complete chore, and I get it; sometimes I am not in the mood to cook either and dominos.co.uk just seems like the right choice. Medium pepperoni with a garlic dip – COME AT ME. But when the time is right and I feel like channelling my inner Nigella, there's something quite enchanting about the process of turning a hunk of raw meat and a handful of vegetables into a stew that puts a smile on the faces of all recipients. Of course, it doesn't always go to plan and I'm often found having a Martine McCutcheon *Love Actually* moment – 'f**k, b******s, s**t' – over a chargrilled fillet of salmon that's reminiscent of my dad's BBQ skills (sorry Dad!), or rice that I haven't cooked for long enough and is like chewing through tiny little shards of rock. *But*, when I have timings on my side and my skills are having an 'on' day, making dinner is the daily routine that helps me switch my work mode and stress level monitor fully off.

A CHILLED-OUT WORKOUT

A high-intensity, 'sweat till you're melting' workout has a time and place, but for moments when I feel like my head might explode with task to-dos where I haven't even scratched the surface, a routine that's slower paced is the perfect antidote for an overstuffed brain. Activities like Pilates, yoga or swimming, or even an outdoor walk, give you a chance to have some time away from your phone, emails, diary – the lot. Plus the emphasis on mindful movement and focus on breathing really do force you to a place where you can't think about much else. If you're used to throwing yourself into a double-digit round of burpees then I can understand that it might sound a little *yawn* to take it so slowly, but 8pm reformer Pilates sessions that finish with a mini-meditation which makes you dribble a little because you're THAT relaxed are rather lovely.

A SCHEDULING SESSION

You know there are some times when you feel like the laws of physics are being defied and your task list is physically weighing down on your shoulders? Yes? I feel you, sister. In those sorts of moments no amount of bath salts or garlic salt sprinkling will solve it. Instead I move onwards with the plan of action that I've created for myself. I open out my Bullet Journal, get up my diary and work on my plans for the week ahead. It's hardly the sexiest stress reliever, but I do find that by having a definitive plan of action down on paper, the chewed-up checklist gets out of my head and into a format that's actually helpful. I'd recommend trying not to waste hours putting a super-detailed to-do list together; instead focus on two or three high-priority tasks that must get done each day, and there's a higher chance that you'll tick them off.

I told you that I'm a traditional kinda gal when it comes to stress relievers. You might not feel like any the five methods I've outlined here are for you. Maybe you like to crash about on your drum kit until the neighbours start hammering a 'FOR SALE' sign into their front lawn? Or perhaps kicking some metaphorical and literal ass at a boxing class is more your style? BUT there is one stress-relieving tactic that everyone, everywhere should deploy regularly. It's time for a digital detox and don't @ me.

HOW TO DEAL WITH ONLINE OVERWHELM

Hello. My name is Anna and I'm addicted to my mobile phone. It comes everywhere with me and at least twice a day I lose it somewhere in the flat and my heart begins to pound at a beat-per-minute rate that I don't even achieve at the gym. I guess that's my cardio sorted. I know I'm not the only one. Growing up with a phone that only had Snake and the function to create your own polyphonic ringtones meant that mobiles didn't occupy the space in our lives that they do now. These days they connect us to the whole world via voice, videos, photos and cute-dog filters. They tell us what the weather is going to be like this afternoon, how many steps we took yesterday (I just checked, 428 – poor effort), if we're on target with our water intake, our current bank balance, how to get from A to B in a new city (CityMapper is LIFE), what the stocks and shares market looks like (least used function ever – surely?) and where the hell our food delivery driver has got to.

So in truth, while our mobile phones are an incredible tool for communication, it's unsurprising that they exacerbate feelings of stress and overwhelm, and that they aid procrastination.

I think we can all collectively agree that we're perhaps a little *too* clingy with our mobiles.

Does one charge of battery not even last a day for you?

Do you pick up your phone constantly, even when there's no notification?

Do you take your phone to the toilet with you? (So gross, but I reckon about 95% of us do this.)

Do you eat while looking at your phone? (Particularly grim when you take into account the toilet point.)

Do you have your phone out when you watch TV?

Do you hold your phone in your hand more than you have it in your bag or a pocket?

If you answered yes to at least two or more of the above questions, welcome to the club.

I recently downloaded the app Moment which tracks the number of pick-ups you do of your phone each day and how long you spend on it in total, and the results were downright gross. (iPhones now track this automatically: swipe left from the home screen to see your screentime figure). During the week I could scroll away for up to six hours a day in total, hunched over and staring at my phone – although this number did decrease to a slightly more digestible one to two hours at weekends and whenever I was away on holiday. Seeing those figures in black and white really helped me to understand just how badly I needed to up my digital detox game, and that it was time to create some space between me and technology. These days I try to aim for two hours a day; plenty of time for me to catch up with friends and complete all relevant work tasks on my mobile, without feeling like I've overdone it. Give Moment a download and after a week of tracking, check in to see what your numbers are looking like. *Now* are you convinced that you need a digital detox right this second?

A digital detox is the idea of going cold turkey on tech for a certain period of time. Yep, that's phones, TV, radio, computers – basically anything that connects us to the outside word – all switched off. It takes you back to being nine again and being banned from watching *Nickelodeon*. What's a gal to do, eh? But the benefits of completing a digital detox, even just for a two-hour stint, are obvious. Any time away from that sleep-zapping, blue-tinted screen means time away from being hassled by emails, texts and WhatsApp groups with 34 participants **shivers**. It means time for you to enjoy hobbies and activities or just have a long ol' nap, without distractions. It's the best way to disconnect, and when you're ready to switch back on to the online world, you'll do so with a bit more buzz in your scroll and energy in your soul.

I partook in my first ever digital detox two years ago. I took one whole Sunday, completely tech-free with my phone switched off in my bedside table. After a shaky start where I slept in until 10am and then was desperate to power it up, I spent the day with my family, playing board games, having a bath that was so long it probably deserves to be in the record books, and flicking through magazines that had been gathering dust on my nightstand and were approximately six months out of date. I slept like a baby and the next day I had this strange, focused feeling that I couldn't quite put my finger on – but it felt flippin' fantastic. Since then a digital detox is something that I've tried to do as often as work and plans permit. Go on, we should all be giving this one a go. I'm not taking any excuses here.

HOW TO COMPLETE A DIGITAL DETOX AND ACTUALLY ENJOY IT

1   SCHEDULE IT IN. Find a day of the week that works best for you (for me that's usually a Sunday), and then add a digital detox to your diary once a month - or however often you plan on un-gluing your phone from your palm - and you'll be much more likely to successfully complete it with that calendar reminder pinging up and staring you back in the face. Once you get in the groove of things, you might even want to go the whole hog and ditch your phone for a 48-hour weekend stint.

2   SAFETY FIRST. Let your nearest and dearest know about your plans and give them your home phone number to contact you if they really need to. Although, do people even have a home phone these days? I'm not sure we've got one. I must check. Either way tell the people who would be most likely to contact you just so they don't panic. I wouldn't worry about sharing your experiment with everyone as you may find that, like me, upon turning your phone on literally no one has messaged you. It's a great wake-up call for the ol' ego too, as it turns out.

Before you begin your digital detox, I'd suggest concocting a plan. A safe bet is to spend the day being social. It's a win–win situation whoever you decide to spend your time with. People like your grandparents or parents, who might only use their iPads for news and weather updates, are good to hang out with if you feel like even just seeing someone with a mobile in their hand is going to push you over the edge. However, hanging out with your mates will be an eye-opening experience that demonstrates just how much time we spend trying to tap out a message mid-conversation on the down-low and referencing photos, memes, GIFs and Google searches in conversations. If it's your first digital detox then it might be an idea to begin with the former and work your tolerance up to a point where you can be in a room full of switched on tech without feeling the need to power up your own.

When your phone-free day actually arrives, it's a good idea to have some old-school activities on hand so that your palms aren't itching for a keypad. Personally I think that board games should never be sniffed at: Scrabble, UNO and Sequence are some family favourites. Baths are also a major win. Light a candle, make a beard out of bubbles and that's your evening sorted right there. Plus there's always the great outdoors to explore; colouring books that you probably got for Christmas and have never used; put pen to paper and start jotting down ideas for that novel you've always wanted to write, or begin drawing that photo you've always wanted to sketch. I also find it a good time to get round to doing things that I've been putting off, like clearing out the loft, writing thank-you cards and organising my photos into photo albums because the pile of pictures was beginning to look like the Leaning Tower of Pisa.

5 HOLD ON! You might find by the end of the day that you haven't missed your mobile at all. *Instagram who?!* If that's the case then why not extend your digital detox by an extra day? But if you're feeling like you might trip up, head to the bedroom and do everything you possibly can to get to sleep. You spray that pillow spray! You do your stretches! You put your legs up against a wall to get your blood flowing or whatever the Yogis say that it does! Once you're 10 minutes into a good book you won't be thinking about what Chrissy Teigen is up to on Twitter. Then when the morning arrives your mind will feel clear and cleansed and any sense of ego that you did have previously will drift away as you turn your phone on and it sits there silent in your palm, notification-less.

Pop this book down for a minute, grab your calendar and add in a digital detox. Go on. I'll wait for you. Yep, you're done? Here's where you got to! Brilliant. Although going without your phone for a prolonged period might seem like some form of self-inflicted torture at first, the more you practise and complete it successfully, the more you'll realise how beneficial this unplugged time is to our mental health and general wellbeing. It gives us the headspace to edit and process our thoughts, and the physical hours on the clock to be fully engaged in whatever it is that we're doing. It's the definition of quality time.

As part of an edited life, not only is there a smorgasbord of benefits to be had from quality time spent doing things that make you happy, but also quality time spent sleeping. In fact, mental health and sleep couldn't be more closely related. Research published by Alvaro et al. in 2017 found that in a group of high-school students, insomnia symptoms predicted symptoms of depression and vice versa. Of course, from anecdotal evidence of that time that you didn't go to sleep till 5am because you were staying at your friend's house for your first ever sleepover, you know that a lack of sleep will make you feel like utter shit. So here's how to get a good night's rest.

You know that classic saying: 'You have the same amount of hours in a day as Beyoncé'? Well, my guess is that Beyoncé isn't the 'lie-in-until-midday' kinda type. As a fellow Virgo, I too am an annoying morning person. You know the ones who are first at the breakfast buffet in a hotel, asking you, 'Did you sleep well last night?', in a manner that is too chirpy for 95% of the population at 6.30am. *Yeah*, that's me. But don't be thinking that I'm a sleep hater just because I like to get up early. In fact, if you were to ask me where my favourite place on earth was I'd probably say my bed. IT'S GREAT. I love sleep, and given my alarm time, I like to make sure I get enough hours in. Trust me, on anything less than about six hours of sleep I'm a TOTAL Grinch.

Mornings are like Marmite. There'll be some night owls out there who have productivity just flowing through their veins at midnight, or those who struggle to drift off into the land of nod, full stop. In that case, feel free to ignore me and lean in to whatever bedtime and morning alarm fits in best with your personal schedule and internal body clocks. Consult your diary, and if your days are loaded to be busier in the mornings and you're struggling to brush your hair while closing the front door behind you, then perhaps it's worth going to bed half an hour earlier and doing the same with your wake-up alarm. Or perhaps you're just not that productive in the morning, and your meetings and socials tend to trickle into your evenings when you're feeling on it, then do a midnight march to bed. It's all about tuning in to your personal energy levels and how they alter throughout the day, and balancing that with the logistical matter of your work, life and social schedules.

Maybe it's just because I'm such a huge fangirl of sleep, but I do feel like this pillar, perhaps even more than any of the other three, is most deeply connected to how you're doing with all the others. If you're managing to get a handle on stress, then you'll sleep better. If you're feeding yourself well and not downing umpteen cups of coffee before bed, then you'll sleep better. If you've incorporated workouts into your weekly routine, then you'll *definitely* sleep better. However, if you do feel like shifting your wake-up time forward a little and you're still struggling to be perky in the morning, even with some editing action on your other self-care pillars, then here's how I execute my evening and morning routines to gear me up to run the world come the AM...

HOW TO BE A MORNING PERSON, WITHOUT BECOMING A ZOMBIE

TIME TO BECOME A GRANNIE

If you can go to bed at 1am and then wake up at 6am then I applaud you. You're either someone who can survive on very little amounts of sleep, or a parent, and either way you have my uttermost respect. I am neither of those things and so in order to get up before lunchtime, I need to be in bed by 10pm and then asleep by 10.30pm or else my alarm will be duly ignored. I find the 'eight hours of sleep a night' rule rings true, and I try to aim for that amount; any longer or shorter and I feel like I have the energy of a sloth when I wake up. I suggest experimenting with different bedtimes and alarms until you find one where it's physically possible to remove yourself from bed in the morning and fits in with your lifestyle, job and routines. If you usually go to bed at 1am and wake up at 9am, then bring both of those times back by 30 minutes and aim to be asleep by 12.30pm and set your alarm for 8.30am. Continue tweaking these times until you find a set-down/wake-up that works with your schedule and leaves you feeling at your most energised.

DO EVERYTHING YOU POSSIBLY CAN TO GET TO SLEEP

If you're someone who stays up until 2am watching Netflix each night, then you may argue that going to sleep at 10pm is beyond the realms of possibility for you. However, there are some tricks that I use to fool my brain and body into thinking that it's time to hit the hay. A hot bath or shower and mini moisturiser massage before getting into your pyjamas will not only leave your limbs looking all J.Lo-esque, but should help to ease any aches and pains. Why do you think that babies love massage so much,

DIY SLEEP SPRAY RECIPE

You will need:
A mini glass bottle with a spray atomiser
10–15 drops of lavender essential oil
30ml vodka
30ml distilled water

Method:
1 Add the essential oils and vodka to the bottle and swirl to blend.
2 Pour in your distilled water, shake to mix and it's ready to spray.

eh? Throw in a body oil that's lavender-scented and you'll be dozing
off in no time. Make sure the room is as dark as it can be (if not, invest
in blackout blinds or curtains) and the temperature is set slightly lower
than you have it during the day. The most time-efficient steps are to
invest in a good 'sleep spray' to mist over your bed linen (look for one
with high-quality essential oil ingredients or make your own – see box),
sink into your pillows with your current read, audiobook or podcast if
you prefer to listen to your literature, and dim the lights in the room at
least 30 minutes before you plan to drift off. It's also a good idea to set
your phone's alarm for the morning, turn it onto silent mode and place
it out of arm's reach before you get ready for this routine. Not only
are these tips good to incorporate day to day, they're also good ones to
bookmark if you need to ward off the jet-lag head fog during travel.

THE NO-SNOOZE RULE

If you're a snoozer in the morning then getting out of this routine will
be the hardest one to break. I have to say that I've never really got into
it myself because the idea of getting an extra nine minutes of sleep
just doesn't appeal. I want another hour, dammit! To resist the urge
to snooze, do whatever you need to do to stay awake. For me that's
scrolling through my phone, which isn't usually the kind of advice that
you find in these books, but I'm a firm believer in editing routines for
yourself. I've tried this whole meditation malarkey and I just end up
nodding off again. Nope, not for me, but it might work for you (the
Headspace and Rituals app are two that I do recommend). I also find
that having my dressing gown and cosy slippers right next to the bed,
especially in the winter months, helps to make the move to freezing
cold duvet-less world a little easier.

CREATE A ROUTINE

Having a set of rituals that you do each morning will help make the
transition from 'morning hater' to 'person who still hates to see dawn
but can see the advantages of getting up a little earlier each day' a tad
smoother. My routine involves me throwing myself out of bed and into
something snuggly, before making the bed (taking away the temptation
to roll straight back into it) and heading into the kitchen to rustle up
some breakfast. Once that's consumed, I take stock of my to-do list for
the day and any events or meetings I have scheduled in, before having
a shower and making myself look presentable while mulling over my
plans. I try to follow this routine most weekdays, and find I'm at my
most productive when I set myself up properly in this way. The main

thing to nail here is the not getting back into bed thing, so for me that means breakfast immediately because I've been thinking about it since 7pm the night before. But perhaps it's best to get straight up and dressed if you bathe in the evenings, or if you're a morning shower-er then there is nothing more refreshing than getting clean first thing. I try my best, but it doesn't *always* run smoothly. Sometimes I can up end up pulling out my laptop and working in bed until the postman comes and I realise that it's almost lunchtime and all I've eaten are some leftover M&S Chocolate Cornflake Mini Bites that I had hanging around.

Speaking of M&S Chocolate Cornflake Mini Bites, which coincidently are now all I want to eat, it's time to have a word about food now that I've dished out every sleep-inducing trick in the book. All the four self-care pillars in *An Edited Life* contribute to both your mental *and* physical wellbeing, but there is something about the consumption of food which makes the relationship between the two a tangible one. IT'S WHAT YOU'RE PUTTING IN YOUR BODY! Feeding yourself well takes time, thought and sometimes a hefty slice out of your budget, but when we physically provide ourselves with the correct nutrients, along with the long-term benefits of that, we can pretty quickly end up feeling in a good place mentally too. Our body feels great, our minds follow, we sleep like a log, we increase our energy for movement and concentration levels for productiveness, and a new sense of confidence takes over. Right, now pass me the Cornflake Mini Bites...

Eating well

I really wish I felt like my best and most energetic self after necking down a whole pizza, but unfortunately that's not the case. You already know the drill here: a varied diet that's heavy on nutritious and fresh whole foods will result in you feeling satisfied and spritely. I'm not a nutritionist, nor a dietitian, so I'll spare you food facts and instead just mention that I'm all for a bit of everything in moderation. I don't restrict my diet in any way, instead trying to tune in to what my body needs and editing my fridge and kitchen cupboards to reflect that. When I feel like I'm completely acing my diet it's because I'm cooking the majority of our meals at home, trying out new recipes and actually enjoying the whole process. By chowing down on veggies and proteins and fats, carbohydrates and fibre, I feel more switched on and prepared for stress, I'm present in my workouts and I fall asleep without feeling like I have a bowling ball stuffed up my top.

Whenever I do order from my local pizza place (which is saved to my favourites, because, you know, #balance), it's because we've planned poorly and are therefore poorly prepared, with no food in the house and absolutely zero impetus to move. I'm guessing that this scenario is a familiar one for most of us. Of course the obvious move here is to begin incorporating meal planning and a subsequent weekly food shop into our routines. Conjuring up an image of soggy vegetables stored away in Tupperware boxes and having to eat meals that we're just not in the mood for is hardly the most appealing of ideas out there. But not only does it keep us on track when it comes to eating well, it slots in easily with budgeting – which means we can eat a healthy and varied diet without needing to remortgage – and it makes prepping and cooking a streamlined process that doesn't demand an endless number of hours in the day.

Being an at-home worker makes meal planning the perfect choice for us because if there's something I need to prep a couple of hours in advance I can slope into the kitchen at lunch, and when it's time to do the weekly food shop I can visit when the rest of the world isn't doing their weekly pilgrimage too. However, it's all about flexibility here and if it's something that you've never tried before then it can seem a bit daunting to have to think about food up to seven days ahead. BUT, just imagine a world where you don't have to pop by the supermarket on your way home from work every night and drop £20, or have to spend the afternoon wondering what the hell you're going to cook for dinner that night? It doesn't have to be that way! Find out how to get the hang of it by turning the page.

1 **BE PREPARED.** If the kitchen is a mess then I often slink in, pour myself a bowl of cereal and remove myself from the situation immediately. The truth is that in order to slice up carrots and whizz up some hummus in your food processor for a snack, you're going to want a clean and organised workspace to do it in. So have a whip around, and, if needed, invest in some key kitchen utensils too.

KITCHEN UTENSIL CHECKLIST:

- Non-stick pans & bakeware
- Good-quality knives
- Measuring cups & spoons
- Food processor and/or blender (I've said many times before that I would happily marry mine as I use it surprisingly often)
- Kitchen scales
- Large non-stick stock pot
- Chopping boards
- Silicone or wooden utensils
- Colander, sieve & grater
- Glass containers with lids (IKEA do great ones)
- Slow cooker (optional, but great!)
- Mixing bowls (metal ones are easy to clean and slim to store)

2 **TIME TO PLAN.** Grab a piece of paper and write the days of the week down the side. Make a note next to it with how many people you're cooking for each evening – the chances are that if there are fewer than usual, you'll be able to make the dinner from the previous day stretch for leftovers. At the top, add in columns for breakfast, lunch and dinner. For ease, I tend to have the same or similar meals for breakfast and lunch each day and mix things up for dinner. If you're a meal-planning newbie then ease yourself in by trying to plan just dinners at first, leaving your breakfast and lunch plans out. In the **Resources** section you'll find the link to a print-off PDF meal-planning template on my blog, or check out Kikki K and Amazon for some great pre-made tear-off pads that magnetise to your fridge. GENIUS.

Before you start thinking of meals, have a look around your kitchen – root around your freezer, get to the back of your cupboards, see what's lurking in your fridge, what spices do you have on your rack? I'm guessing you came across a dusty tin of baked beans and an exploded pack of rice that you'll be finding the remnants of all over your kitchen for the next 20 years of your life, yes? Aside from that, hopefully there will be some food items that need using up, and that's where your inner Delia comes out to play...

Sometimes at home we cook off-the-cuff, but often we use recipes. This is probably because I grew up with my mum religiously leafing through her well-loved 1980s M&S cookbook. Of course there are cookbooks (my most used are *Get the Glow*; *Ready, Steady Glow* and *A Year of Beautiful Eating*, all by Madeleine Shaw), but make sure you save recipes on Instagram or Pinterest that you fancy making, or bookmark posts online. I still like an old-school recipe card from the supermarket too, and I keep all of them along with written or photocopied recipes in a plastic wallet, so they're easy to flick through. Like mother, like daughter. If you haven't got time to then it's a good idea to have a list of around 10–15 recipes that you all enjoy eating and that you can cook up quickly, just so you've got it to hand if you're short on time. Also, have a go-to meal formula for days when you can't be arsed to think of something fancy. For us that's a fish fillet with slices of lemon or miso paste on top, grilled Mediterranean veg with lots of paprika and garlic seasoning, sweet potato wedges and some kind of greens. Simple, filling and doesn't require a recipe.

Once you've got your meal plan down, it's time to write a shopping list. If you have the time, it's worth writing your list in the order that you plan to add items into your trolley. It sounds like a chore, but before I used to do this I always ended up forgetting to buy eggs. FLIPPIN' EGGS! Instead of your usual supermarket set-up, start at the back of the store and first shop home-cleaning supplies, before moving on to dry goods, back through fresh fruit and veg at the front, then to your dairy and meat sections and finishing off with the frozen aisles. It's an odd way to navigate the store, but it means your Ben & Jerry's ice cream won't be the consistency of milkshake once you get home. Although, YUM. Once you've written your list, stick to it. Like really, actively put your blinkers on and tick through your items without giving a second thought to any extras, and NEVER go shopping hungry – eat something before you leave

if you're feeling peckish, otherwise it won't end well for you or your bank balance. Make sure your peripheral vision is ignored when it comes to ends of aisles especially, as that's where the deals and offers tend to lure you in.

6 THE PREP.

After you're home, you've packed everything away and had a quick lie-down because bringing all those bags into the house is quite the workout; then if you've got 30 minutes to spare, prepping is always a good idea. I don't tend to prep anything more than a day in advance because, as I previously mentioned – '*soggy vegetables*', but I do try to make some kind of sweet snack as I inevitably will crave a bar of chocolate at 3pm every day. I usually make some kind of dry fruit/protein ball concoction and stick 'em the fridge for when I'm feeling peckish. With those ready to go and all the ingredients purchased for the week ahead, I'm no longer the pizza place's most loyal customer.

It's not part of the six-step process here, but it's worth noting that we tend to meal plan in our household from Monday to Friday only. I'd spin you a line about how '*it's better for the budget*' to visit the supermarket once a week, but the truth is that, like everyone, I can get lazy. Therefore I try to ACE meal planning Monday to Friday, but come the weekend I just fancy walking down the road for brunch, sloping off for a pub lunch or wangling us an invite to my parents for a Mum-cooked meal. If we have to do a weekend dash to the supermarket to pick up some essentials, then that's fine, but overall I don't worry about planning for Saturday or Sunday. Plus it helps to take the pressure off a little. It's either leftovers or Mum's lasagne.

A SAMPLE MEAL PLAN

	BREAKFAST	LUNCH	DINNER
Monday (both in)	Apple & cinnamon porridge	Homemade soup (stored in the freezer so it keeps for yonks)	Chilli (big batch for leftovers) with rice, guacamole & sour cream
Tuesday (both in, but doing a late Pilates class, so quick dinner)	Apple & cinnamon porridge	Avocado on toast (leftover avocado from yesterday)	Homemade soup (quick and easy to reheat after our workout)
Wednesday (both in)	Apple & cinnamon porridge	Chilli (stored in the freezer from leftovers) with rice	Salmon with Mediterranean vegetables and greens
Thursday (both in)	Apple & cinnamon porridge	Homemade soup (stored in the freezer so it keeps for yonks)	Veggie burgers with homemade sweet potato chips
Friday (just me)	Apples & yoghurt (use up leftover yoghurt that Mark hasn't eaten)	Avocado on toast with an egg (avocados about to go off!)	Chilli (stored in the freezer from leftovers) with rice

MONEY-SAVING MEAL-PLANNING TIPS

Seeing as eating well isn't always the cheapest way to get food in your gob, here are my top 10 tips for making good food fit into your budget and last well so that you don't end up with mouldy food in your fridge that looks like it could be part of some kind of modern art installation:

- Frozen fruit and veg is the cheapest way to get some greenery in your diet. Frozen veg is so quick and easy to heat up and frozen fruit can easily be added to your morning porridge to thaw it out, or into a smoothie for a fraction of the price of the fresh version.

- A well-stocked store cupboard is a game changer and can turn a humble potato into a smoky BBQ paprika-spiced potato wedge with just a few grinds and shakes. It's an investment at first, but make sure you have salt, pepper, olive oil, red wine vinegar, soy sauce, garlic granules, paprika, cumin, chilli powder, cinnamon, oregano and mustard (I like wholegrain) as your basics, and add to them as you please.

- Mouldy bread was a permanent fixture in our kitchen cupboards until I discovered this tip: place two slices of bread (or however many you use in a day) in a sandwich bag in the fridge and stuff the rest of your loaf in the freezer. When you've used up the slices in the fridge, replace with more from the freezer. No more mould! MAGIC.

- If there's a good deal on meat or fish then you know what to do (my local supermarket does amazing 'Fish Friday' bargains). Just put the packs in the freezer on the day of purchase and defrost in the fridge the night before you're planning on using it. Do not repeat this process, and eat the frozen goods within a month.

- You can freeze cheese too! Who knew? It changes the texture so it's not the best if you're planning on getting fancy with a cheeseboard or eating it in a sandwich, but it still works great for cooking. Just pre-cut the cheese before you store the chunks in a sandwich bag in the freezer, and take out the piece you need the day before to defrost.

- Bags of salads and leafy greens are notorious for turning into slime in a matter of hours. Instead, wash the leaves or half-eaten bags of salad and place them in a sandwich bag with a paper towel that helps to mop up all the moisture. They should then last two days.

How many times have I mentioned sandwich bags here? They're super-handy for a lot of things around the house, but especially in the kitchen. I put chopped up onions and herbs in them, individual portions of leftovers, meat or fish for the freezer, and they're handy for storing half of a fruit or vegetable in for later.

Usually I'd throw eggs into the 'buy in bulk' mantra, but eggs taste best within two weeks of purchase. So if you find that they're sitting in your fridge for longer than that before they all get eaten, buy smaller quantities more frequently.

If the contents of the vegetable drawer of your fridge have seen better days, then chop everything up, roast in the oven with some oil, salt and pepper and spices, then throw into your food processor with a few glugs of veggie stock to thin it out into a soup. That's tomorrow's lunch right there. Pour into individual tubs or sandwich bags and store in the freezer for the next time you fancy a winter warmer.

It's not necessarily money-saving per se, but weekly food box delivery services like HelloFresh and Gusto are a good idea for those of us out there who just don't have the time or impetus to get behind meal planning. Most services come in at a couple of pounds more expensive per head than if you were to source the ingredients yourself, but it does cut down on possible leftover waste, is so convenient and there are always voucher codes to snap up online.

With your food consumption planned and prepped and no longer sucking away time and money on the way home from work, it's time to incorporate the final pillar of self-care – physical activity. You've planned to have a quick and easy dinner after your evening spin class and so now it's time to actually go. With the tweaks that you've made to improve your mental health, sleep and diet, your body should be ready to move and your mind in a place where it doesn't think that working up a sweat is the most horrible idea that it's ever heard. The truth is that the advantages of adding a frequent workout routine to your life are *endless*. An increase in strength, muscle mass and blood flow during high-activity periods is the endorphin-induced cherry on top of the self-care pie. In case you need a little more convincing, we're deep-diving in…

We all remember watching Mr Motivator on morning TV and so it should come as no shock that physical activity should be high up on our to-do lists, although sometimes there is nothing that I want to do in the world less than working out. In fact, I'd rather eat coriander-laden avocado toast (side note: coriander is the devil's herb). However, not only are there the obvious physical benefits to working out, more importantly there are often mental ones too, and in the context of self-care, *that's* what we should really be using to give ourselves a kick up the ass.

Sure, it can be pretty rank. The sweat patches that make it look like your top has turned a whole different colour. The instant regret whenever you wear something that's grey. The way that burpees can make you feel like you're never going to be able to breathe without wheezing ever again. Despite all that, a workout – burpee-filled or not – can make you feel a hormone high that's unmatched. It forces us to have an hour away from our phones, like a mini digital detox, and mentally log out from whatever is going on at home, at work, or in life. Your mind pushes aside the day's stresses and instead focuses on whether it's normal to last just three seconds in the plank position. I'm telling you, once you edit in a workout routine that fits for you, you'll practically be skipping home. *If you can still feel your hamstrings…*

HOW TO FIND A ROUTINE

Some might view routines as a boring and yawn-inducing construct that confines us to times and activities that are difficult to break out of. And yes, that's true for some and it might be time for my husband and me to actually head out of the flat on a Saturday night instead of looking at each other, each raising an eyebrow and then one of us going to grab the laptop to order takeaway. But a routine here is something that's going to hold you accountable and help to get you in the swing of things and provide structure and motivation in the early days when you're finding your feet with this whole '*move more*' thing.

My exercise routine currently consists of reformer Pilates and reformer Pilates with a side order of more reformer Pilates, although I've previously given a bit of everything a go. Me, a creature of habit? NEVER. I had an 18-month stint with a personal trainer where I developed a butt. I completed daily yoga sessions in my front room that I found on YouTube and found peace in downward dog. I joined my dad for a spin class and realised that it was possible to sweat out your entire water content in just 45 minutes. I did a barre class that made me realise that I have all the elegance of a staggering newborn lamb. I once got into running, but then developed shin splints that left me crying mid-run and my dad had to come and collect me in the car and drive me home (I must admit that was a low point). All these things made me sweat, puff, but overall made me feel *good*, although the ones that stuck the longest were the activities that I enjoyed most.

And that's the point to hammer home here. A fitness routine only ever sticks when you enjoy it. If the idea of peeling yourself out of bed to trek into the freezing cold to the gym makes you physically recoil (kudos to you if it doesn't), then the chances are that you'll pull out every excuse in the book in order to wriggle your way out of it. Of course there will be days when the last thing you want to do is a workout, but if 80% of the time you're up for your chosen method of exercise, then it's all good.

So how do you find the right sweat sesh for you? Well, firstly do some head scratching. Is there something that you've done in the past that you've lost touch with that you'd like to start up again? Do you find yourself yearning to run when a runner swooshes past you on the pavement? Are your mates raving about a new class they think you'd love (my friend once tried to convince me to attend a class that was quite literally a rave)? Is there a studio that you pass every day on the way to work that looks like it could be up your street? Basically, you want to gather up all this information, do some Googling and see what floats your boat. Over the page are some workouts that I've tried over the years:

AERIAL YOGA yoga performed in a low-hanging silk, a bit like a hammock. Ok, this is very, very fun indeed. More of a good stretch and a confidence builder in the fact that the silk isn't going to fall down, but perhaps not best for those who suffer with motion sickness.

BARRE a mix of Pilates, dance and yoga moves mainly performed on a classic ballet barre. The workout that made me realise that elegance is not something I possess, but boy did I struggle to sit down without pain the next day.

BOOTCAMP a functional training class that's usually outside, using bodyweight moves and outdoor equipment. A great choice for those who love being shouted at while they work out (I bizarrely do) and don't mind getting a bit muddy in the process. Got to love the great outdoors.

BOXING a full body burn using the techniques and exercises that boxers use to train, but prepare for more than just punching. Toughest. Workout. EVER. Makes you feel like a badass.

CLUBBERCISE an aerobic workout performed to some dance bops, all while you wave around glowsticks. I did this with my mum and her friends and I don't think I've ever laughed so hard. The glowsticks are worth the class fee alone.

HIKING walking up a hill because you actually want to, not because your parents are making you do it. In my old age I actually really like a good hike, and if you live in the countryside or just an area that's nice to walk around, it's a free and low-impact way to get moving.

MUAY THAI the national sport of Thailand that incorporates close combat moves, some performed with a sparring partner. Screw the above. THIS is the toughest. Workout. EVER. I actually sweated out of my eyeballs when I did this.

REFORMER PILATES: a mix of moves that promote length, strength and flexibility all performed on the reformer machine created by Joseph Pilates. My current love, for the fact that it involves SO much lying down and has led to me being able to touch my toes for the first time since I was a limber little toddler.

RESISTANCE TRAINING: weight training that specialises in using resistance to build strength, muscle and anaerobic endurance. As tough as you want to make it, but the results I saw from doing it regularly felt pretty incredible. I HAD AN ASS. It may have only been for a short period of time, but it felt great while it lasted.

RUNNING: you put one foot in front of the other and move like someone is shouting 'RUN FOREST! RUN!' at you. It's free! Plus it's easy to find people to run with and adapt into your schedule.

SPINNING: indoor cycling that focuses on endurance, performed on a stationary bike. You've probably got the gist by now that I'm a prolific sweater, but spinning causes me to produce record amounts.

SWIMMING: an activity that makes your hair wet every time even if you invest in the best swimming cap in the world. One for people who don't mind washing their hair every day. I am not one of those people.

YOGA: a physical, mental and spiritual practice that originated in ancient India. A relaxing method of working out that is surprisingly tough. I felt bendy and super-chilled when I checked in with it regularly.

Once you've got a few solid ideas, have a look at your schedule and see where you'll realistically be able to edit them in. 'I don't have time!' is the excuse I pulled out for years, despite being child-free and self-employed – PAH! – but I reckon about 99.95% of us out there *do* have the time, even if it's just for a one-hour session once a week. It's about finding those pockets that you're currently wasting on activities that don't particularly nourish you in any way. The hour spent scrolling on your phone before you get out of bed, the evenings spent watching *Friends* episodes back-to-back that you've seen approximately 76 times, the lunch break where you find yourself flicking through Twitter but not reading anything at all. Start small and work to increase your sessions as you enjoy it more and begin to see results. Try and aim to stick to some kind of routine for at least a month. Then when you've powered through, take a look back and see if there were any days where you ended up being late for a meeting, where you were too sore from the workout before, or if the 6am class just felt like hell to you – evaluate, adjust and sweat it for the next month. Oh, hello? What's that? A routine that's just snuck up on you without you even realising.

You know that annoying phrase that gets bandied about online? '*You never regret a workout*' – it annoyingly rings pretty true. I mean there was that time that my mate and I joined in a Muay Thai class and she ended up in hospital with a twisted knee, but on the whole I've ended more workouts feeling knackered and weirdly energised than I have in the waiting area of A&E. If it's not only time, but also money that's putting a roadblock in the way of working out, then why not grab a friend who's into running to take you out for a jog on one of their routes? Or invite your mate round at the weekend and tell her to bring a yoga mat so you can both stretch out to a video in your front room as you gossip (a thick towel makes a good replacement for a mat, especially on a carpeted floor). Maybe your other half is a mad-for-it gym bunny who could do some circuit training drills with you in the local park? It doesn't have to cost the world, it doesn't have to take up hours and hours of your week and it doesn't have to completely suck balls. *Promise.*

HOW TO STICK TO IT

So you've worked out your plan of action, you're actually doing it, you (sometimes) enjoy it – how do you make it stick? And by stick I mean last longer than a month-long flash in the pan 'New Year, New Me' fitness fad. Well, I have some ideas…

I always thought that I was a solitary sweater. I only ever perspired alone or with my PT (who said that I was his second sweatiest client – second only to a burly bloke who could deadlift twice his own body weight). I thought my lack of coordination and ability to sound like a squeaky toy as I struggle to breathe after running for just one minute would leave me flailing around at the back of the class. However, I've realised that even though I am in fact right about both of those things, it DOESN'T MATTER. No one actually cares if you have to wipe down your reformer Pilates machine after the warm up because there are actual beads of sweat on there. Everyone is too focused on their own game, and if you are struggling, they're around to give words and whoops of encouragement if needed. Plus it's a chance to break out of your usual social circles and make some new mates. As someone who works for herself and has little interaction aside from with the postman each morning, I've found the act of getting proper clothes on (well, *lycra*), leaving the house and making small talk with others is perhaps even more beneficial than my new and improved hamstring flexibility.

So you remember your slick and newly organised calendar? Once you get the hang of inputting meetings, deadlines and appointments in there, try scheduling in your workouts too. I add my reformer Pilates sessions in my personal diary, but just as I would any other meetings – with timings and a reminder set for the day before. This way, not only do you not forget them and it's easy to change things around when you end up putting your back out trying to do the worm on your one night out past 11pm, it also labels them with *priority* – which is something that we don't tend to attribute to workouts. We book them in, use up credits, and then when the session comes around and we've spent the day trying to keep afloat amongst a packed-out diary (we'll get to solving that later), the first thing that gets bumped off the agenda is a dip in the pool after work to do some lengths. Sometimes we're not physically up to a workout and that's ok. Sometimes our time might be better spent elsewhere, and that's ok too. But nine times out of ten, it will only be beneficial to drag our arses to the gym and DO IT, so giving workouts this level of priority in our diary should help us to hit that success rate.

As materialistic as it sounds (and is!), sometimes the only thing that can motivate me to jump back into my routine is a new outfit. It's not exactly in line with my capsule wardrobe ethos, but a brand-spanking new pair of leggings or a sports bra that somehow manages to manoeuvre my flat chest into a cleavage *and* give support, can give me the impetus to get back on it, even if it's just because I want to take my new gear out for a ride. It makes us feel good and feel confident in a way that I just can't seem to summon if I go to the studio in an ill-fitting pair of baggy leggings and one of my old hole-ridden PJ t-shirts. Plus we do actually need the correct kit. There is nothing worse than a chafing seam on a pair of leggings, let me tell you. We put this genre of clothing fully through its paces – stretching, rubbing and washing them on intense and scalding cycles – so it's only common sense that from time to time we might need to start from scratch. Here's what I look for:

Sports bra
For those gifted in the chest area, look for high support with adjustable straps and front fastening. Across the board, we should all seek out styles with minimal or concealed seams; check for any possible scratchy areas by swinging your arms as if you are running in the changing room.

T-shirt
Thin, sweat-wicking fabrics will keep you cooler during your workout, and stop your top from sticking and clinging to you as you pump iron. It's important you feel comfortable in your kit, but slightly slimmer-fitting tops won't ride up as you do any moves that involve you bending over. HELLO DOWNWARD DOG!

Leggings
A high-quality legging is definitely something that's worth investing in. Look for sweat-absorbing, breathable fabrics and fits with a high but soft waistband to give you support around your core. Be sure to give them a good test by lunging and squatting and checking for coverage and any uncomfortable areas.

Trainers
Your choice of footwear is going to be dependent on whatever sport you've decided to take up and how your foot moves when you walk, run or train. My only advice? If you take up running then PLEASE get fitted for footwear by a professional. Your shins, calves, glutes, hamstrings and basically your whole body will thank you for it.

BOOK IN ADVANCE

As I said before, there's something about the act of booking into a class that I've realised helps me to stay accountable when it comes to my fitness routine. It's partly because I'm a people-pleaser who doesn't want to let anyone down, but also because often there's a chunk of cash on the table that just gets flushed down the loo if I don't attend. If running home with your mate after work or joining in a free bootcamp session at the weekend is working for you, then sweat away. However, I've found that paying for sessions (especially those that have a strict 24-hour cancellation policy) has meant that if I've booked in for a session then I'm GONNA GO: I don't want my money to go to waste. My direct debit list doesn't make for dreamy bedtime reading, but it's the whole '*invest in yourself*' motto, which I can 100% get behind. Just factor your classes into your budget and you'll be a-ok.

BE FLEXIBLE

I love routines (the author of a book about life organisation likes to stick to a rigid schedule? SHOCKER). And while I think it's important to settle into some kind of rhythm with fitness if possible, sometimes the beat is going to go a little off and that's where flexibility needs to kick in. Perhaps it's worth setting a number of sessions that you'd like to complete over a two-week cycle. Say five gym workouts every two weeks. Make a tick-list in your diary for each session and then cross it off whenever you have the chance to complete it. You're not tied down to a Monday, Wednesday and Friday grind that might just not jive with you, and when your schedule gets thrown in the air, your workout routine doesn't land and roll across the floor, never to be picked up again. Sometimes I find myself booking onto classes with new instructors and actually bloody love them; learning new moves, picking up tips on my form, reaching limits that I didn't think were possible. Next time there's a bump in the road, dust yourself off quickly and you might just find something extra special.

SWITCH IT UP

If all else fails, mix it up. If the fire in your belly for your routine is nothing more than a smoking pile of ash then you're ready to move on. It's exactly what happened to me. After 18 months of seeing my PT three times a week and working on my deadlift skills and squats, it just wasn't floating my boat any more. So I began to incorporate reformer into my routine, and six months later my gym membership was a thing of the past. I loved the Pilates studio I went to so much that I'd have decked myself out in their merch head to toe. Take a step back and leap into something new. It might just be a simple case of changing up your days and trying a new instructor, or maybe you've just done your gym routine 568 times and you need to up your weights and search for some new moves online. Or ditch your current routine completely and take up something new that you've never tried before. Rock climbing! Circus skills! Upside-down yoga taught from a big hammock that hangs off the ceiling! Don't knock it till you've tried it.

The Edit

See? Self-care is about way more than the luxury bath salts and the cashmere socks. In fact it encapsulates so much about what is important for an edited life. Why are we being so hard on ourselves? Getting bogged down with stress, not sleeping well, feeding our bodies with junk and reaching record lows for our daily step-count. The crazy thing is that we do all these things and still expect ourselves to function at a level that's impossible to do when you're running on empty. If we just take a couple of hours out of our weeks, or minutes out of our days, to check ourselves and mentally run through the four pillars I've outlined here – mental health, sleep, eating well and physical activity – and tick through an act or two that we're doing/have done/plan to do that tackles each one, then we should be able to maintain our happy level of self-care service.

Of course, these four plates are never going to be spinning at the same rate and with the same success all the time. The odd bit of ceramic is going to smash every now and again, and when it does don't be hard on yourself: take a breath and slowly start to put the pieces back together. Maybe it's talking to a mate about a problem at work, making your own bedtime blend of sleep spray, cooking up all your almost-mouldy veg into a soup for lunch tomorrow or going for a rambling walk where you end up getting a little lost on your lunch break; all these activities combined or executed individually will act as the glue to repair and bring a smidge of self-care back into your life.

Whereas other chapters in this book focus on streamlining and automating processes, I say take whatever self-care you can. Lap it up in whatever way works for you, prioritise it and never feel guilty for taking time for yourself. With your own health and happiness as the major priority in your life, you might find that others need to be re-jigged a bit. Family is up there, and work – you're on it, but your social life? *insert crickets sound effect* Finding it tough to juggle that one too? Well you don't have to have balls flying all over the place. Here's how...

How to have a social life that works for you

Time with friends and family should be enjoyable and not a logistical nightmare that increases your stress levels just thinking about it. Here's how best to spend and arrange your non-working hours.

When we're younger we spend around seven solid hours a day at school with our friends. We learn together, we play together, we spend our computer credits in the library printing out song lyrics to cover our exercise books together. Then we come home, pick up the phone and spend the period till dinner time nattering to one or two of our mates, talking inanely about boys and how we are going to try wearing concealer as lipstick tomorrow at school. Of course *after* dinner it was time for a couple of hours on MSN (or as lengthy as you could make it until your parents needed to use the phone), trying to coincide appearing online at the same time as your crush and then changing your icon to 'BUSY' to appear aloof. The point here is that we spend our child and teenage lives constantly being or in communication with our mates. Our worlds revolve around our social lives because it's a big part of us learning the skills we need to interact with others, and it isn't until exams are completed, school books packed away never to see daylight again, the dissertation filed, that the focus shifts from your social life and onto your work one.

Not clubbing with your friends on a Monday, Wednesday, Thursday and Friday night is part-and-parcel of graduating from further education, and although your liver and overdraft might thank you for it, when our social lives go from a 100 to like, 5, something has to budge. This isn't going to be the case for everyone, but I feel like, as you wade through your twenties, the night out invites start to dwindle and you and your mates get flaky with plans because you're 'snowed under with emails/had a NUTS week/had to bring work home with you/*insert new excuse here*'. Work gets stressful (although surely you're as zen as you've ever been after reading the previous chapter?), and adult responsibilities start to mount up, so we go into automatic shutdown mode and cut back on all and any extracurricular activities. Along with the after-work gym session, the girls' night dinner can find itself being cut too.

Now, I'm all for getting your sweat on, but I'd go out on a limb and say that keeping your relationships strong is preferable to getting strong buttocks. As we get older our social circles can get smaller and more tight-knit as we get our heads down with the daily grind. It's also the time where we start to get serious with relationships, so often female friendships can get put on the back burner. Both are common problems that are easily solved when we push them to the forefront and tackle them head on. With less opportunity to grow our circles and constantly meet fresh faces, we really need to work with what we've already got.

When was the last time you planned or hosted a dinner? See! It's been too long. Here's a task that you can implement right this second:

Take a quick breather from this book, head online to doodle.com and begin to create a Doodle poll (a site where you and your mates can add in dates that you're free and see when everyone else is too).

You can name the event, add the location and any notes. Select the dates and times that you're free and then add in your friends' email addresses so they'll be notified and able to select what day and time slots work for them.

Opt for the most popular choice and there you go, girls' night out is back ON.

Time spent with friends is the best use of minutes in my eyes. You know by now that I'm a lover of a solitary sit on the sofa with a good book, but social juice freshly squeezed from mates is needed just as much. They make you laugh and cry. They make you nostalgic and remember times gone by. They share jokes so funny that you think you might need to start paying attention to those Tena Lady commercials. It's basically the fifth pillar of self-care that buoys you up for whatever life tries to throw at you next. In the context of an edited life, time with friends and family can be a great reliever of stress, a solver of almost any issue and a safe place to discuss your thoughts, feelings and plans with those who know you best and might have some handy advice on the matter. It's a chance to be authentically you, which might not happen as often as you'd like – and that's why it's something to not let fall by the wayside.

We all know mates are great – we've got the matching Topshop blazers and everything – but how the hell are we supposed to pin down social gatherings when our diaries are already looking like a game of Tetris?

Over the page you'll find some shorter-term social life fixes, but the reality is that it's important to water these relationships to maintain and protect them in the long run. From my experience, as long as you're checking in with the other person regularly and they know that you're there for them whenever they need you, as they are for you, then there's not too much watering to do. However, I do like sending small tokens, notes or gifts just to say hello!/you're great/I'm thinking of you, without it being because I've done something wrong. Sometimes it's a bunch of flowers, a postcard or a book that I've heard my friend say that they'd love to read and was already on my bookshelf. Other times it's some homemade cakes or a pair of earrings that I've seen in a store that I just know my friend would LOVE. If the budget allows, buying the odd gift here and there or even just sending a card is a really nice touch; it gives you all the gift-giving feels and is the grown-up equivalent of bringing an Elizabeth Duke 'BFF' friendship bracelet into school for your bestie.

A healthy social life should include catch-ups and activities with friends that ultimately leave you feeling good. It shouldn't feel stressful or forced and it certainly shouldn't be making you unhappy. If you are feeling that way, then perhaps it's time to do some friendship editing. Time is precious and we should be using it wisely, having fun and feeling like our best selves. Breaking up is never easy, but letting go of those who are holding you back and being both a mental and physical drain will allow you a chance to cut those ties and set yourself free. I'M A BIRD! Free for opportunities to meet new people, do new things, and spend whatever time you do have doing things that make you feel flipping fab.

FIVE TIPS TO PERK UP YOUR SOCIAL LIFE TODAY

Food with friends is a classic, and it's one that we crack out often in our friendship group. We usually think of catching up with others in the evenings, which can easily get gobbled up by a few exercise classes, a nightmare of a commute home or working late, but there are plenty of other mealtimes to slot social stuff into. You're going to be eating breakfast, lunch *and* dinner anyway, so why not invite your mates round or out for feeding time? It doesn't have to be a big event. If you can squeeze in a breakfast date before work then find a spot that's slap bang in the centre of all your commutes. Lunch breaks are another good time to meet if you work nearby, or are freelance. Plus, they force you to take your full hour and switch off for *real*. We take it in turns to host dinners, sharing out the load and splitting the snacks, main, sides and dessert between the four of us, which means that one person doesn't get lumbered with having to do all the cooking and the hefty food shop cost. Get on your group WhatsApp and get the next *Come Dine With Me* session in.

Once you have assembled the troops, book in your next social with them while you're all there with your diaries accessible. Head to the cinema! Play crazy golf! Do a dinner again! Whatever the occasion, try to pin it down, as it's always nice to know when your next catch-up is and it avoids the whole 'I can do Monday, Wednesday and Friday next week', 'Well I can only do Friday between 5pm and 7pm' organising conversation from hell (but seriously, convert your mates to Doodle and thank me later).

If your schedules are all pretty routine, then you could always try doing something regularly. Maybe you always do dinner on the first Monday of every month? Or perhaps there's a local pub quiz on a Wednesday night that you've always wanted to do. You could start a book club. The book you're reading now could be your first topic *nudge,

nudge, wink, wink*. It's fun to make traditions with your friends, too. Along with some of our old university pals, we do a 'Faux-Mas' every year, which is our fake version of Christmas before everyone gets sucked into family duties. We take it in turns each year to host, and again, each bring a dish. Or try to travel each August bank holiday to somewhere new or do a road trip? Maybe your friendship formula is too routine? If that's the case, then here's an idea from a mate. Every few months she hosts a dinner party, but invites only one friend from each of her different social circles (e.g. her childhood best friend, her uni mate and a colleague), asking each one to bring one of their own friends. Everyone goes knowing someone, so the idea isn't *completely* terrifying, but it's a chance to meet new people that you already have a common link with, and who might just end up being your new BFF.

It's a pretty standard thing for everyone's lives to move at different speeds. Or maybe all your friends are popping out babies and you're still enjoying the Tinder game, or are you the one that's had the baby and needs to increase your mum-friend quota? It might be worth reconnecting with an old acquaintance who looks like they might be in the same boat as you. Social media makes it so easy to keep in touch these days, and I'm sure there's an old school pal of yours whose Instagrams you're always tapping like on, and who is always commenting back on yours – so ask them out for brunch one weekend. Who can turn down brunch, *eh*?

If you find yourself in a place where mates are a bit hard to come by – either through life or distance getting in the way – then get back on the friendship horse and ride your way to a new friendship group. Again, social media is your new BFF (for now). Give the Bumble BFF app a go and connect with local ladies who have the same interests as you, and search online for local groups and classes that you can head to where the room will be packed with like-minded individuals. Introduce yourself. Swap numbers. Give good hugs goodbye! HELLO SOCIAL BUTTERFLY!

If all socials are beginning to feel like a drag, then perhaps it's not your friends that are the problem, maybe it's that you just have too much on during the week.

If your diary is bulging with non-work events and you're struggling to find the next free evening in your calendar, then it's time to reassess. The real red flag here is when everything in your diary is leaving you with a feeling of dread, even occasions that you would normally look forward to (for me that's holding new babies, watching a Ryan Gosling film at the cinema even if it's another *Blade Runner* film, and anything to do with food).

In that case, it's time to start saying no…

The importance of saying no

There's an underlying current that usually runs through this genre of tomes that 'YES' is the magic word. It opens up doors and allows us to turn our hand to new experiences and adventures. Now, that's great and all, but let's remember what happened in *Super Size Me* when the guy had to keep saying yes to upgrade his already gigantic burger to one that could feed a family for a week? It's not *always* the right thing to do. I'm not barging in being the anti-fun police here, but there are some occasions where it's totally cool and actually beneficial for you and your wellbeing to politely decline. In fact I'm a big believer in 'HELL NO'. *Sometimes…*

'Would you be able to make it to my sister's cousin's best friend's 18th birthday party?'

'Oh she's having an amazing baby shower! I know you only met her once back on a night out 10 years ago, but she'd love you to come. Here's the link to her gift registry at Harrods.'

'The hen party is going to be NUTS. There's 30 people going and it's going to cost you £400 and it doesn't include accommodation, but she says she'd love to catch up with you after all these years!'

'I know it's been yonks, but my mum's workmate's daughter would love to "pick your brain" about starting your own business on Sunday. Do you think you'd be able to take her out for lunch?'

You get the gist? There's no one rule that can easily determine what your response to any given choice should be, but there is a simple way to break it down. There are no specifics, it's more a mix of a gut feeling – which thanks to regular bouts of IBS, I actually feel pretty in tune with. Consult your now fully functioning diary and budget to see what's actually feasible. It's an editing process by which the more you listen internally to your gut and get used to comparing that against your time and money plans, the easier it will become. In the confines of your social life it's about deciding whether an interaction or event is right for YOU. Need me to be your Magic 8-Ball for a moment? Here's my quickie decision-making guide to use until you've found your gut:

Do you deep down
actually want to go?

Does the plan fit
with your budget?

Does the invite come
from a close relative
or friend, or someone
you owe a favour to?

Is the time available
in your diary?

Go ahead!
Accept and
add it to your
calendar so you
don't forget

Decline and
send a gift or
note instead

Politely
decline
– NOPE
THANKS!

Ask if there's an alternative activity you
could do that's cheaper or at a different
time, or you actually fancy doing

In the examples on p.94, you're giving your time (and sometimes money) to situations where it may not be reciprocated. Perhaps the invite fills you with panic and you can't think of anything worse than dragging yourself to the 18th birthday party of someone who you don't even know. Or you actually just need to take a day out for some self-care, so you send a gift voucher and a card to the baby shower holder instead. You decline the hen party as the cost will send your budget all over the shop – plan to catch up for some drinks with the hen instead; and for your mum's workmate's daughter you ask to meet for a coffee on a Saturday afternoon when you'll be in town anyway.

The thing to remember here is that YOU are in control of your social life. Although I understand there'll be friend and family engagements that you might just have no other choice but to go to, there will also be plenty of other things in your diary where you do have a choice.

It's not about being a villainous decliner of invites, but more about moulding them into situations where both parties are happy with the outcome, or in cases where that's not always possible – putting yourself as the priority. Oh my word, did I just suggest being *SELFISH*?! Yes. Yes, I did.

Now, actually, I was lying earlier because there are two methods to try here.

Firstly, the next time you find yourself on the receiving end of an invite, ask yourself if you had to go and attend it RIGHT THIS SECOND, would you be up for it? Of course, this question is flawed because you can bet your bottom dollar that if I received my best mate's wedding invite as I was about to spend some sweet sweet time sleeping in bed, then I'd struggle to heave myself out of it, but it's a tactic that's easy to gauge.

The other method is to give yourself a 'free night' quota to fill each week. So for you that might be two nights a week that you tell yourself are all yours – no plans or commitments. Work with the figure until you find one that doesn't make you feel like a hermit, but still gives you enough time to cook yourself a nice meal and watch a Netflix documentary on the sofa. Sometimes it's helpful to have a bit of a ruler to measure things by and I have to say that both these ideas have helped me in the past to curate a social life that's fulfilling for all involved, and in no way creeps into the realm of overwhelm.

There are many aspects of life that are out of our control – that weekly team meeting you have to attend at work every Monday, the fact that coffee shop chains serve extremely watery hot chocolates which is just not great news for us coffee haters – but your social life is something that is completely in your hands. It's up to you. Spend time with those whose company you enjoy and who participate in a two-way friendship; spend less or no time at all with those who don't. *It's simple – you're the editor.*

In terms of actually fitting in your social life, saying no is going to be your new best mate. By declining events you really don't want to go to, you free up space to spend time doing things that you're bloody mad for. Your lunch breaks and evenings will be open to see people during the week (I know, are we students again?!) and your weekends won't be spent in a car trekking to a hen party that's four and a half hours away, when you haven't actually had a proper conversation with the bride for five years. Your social life self-care will be off the charts and the chances are that you'll feel happier and more relaxed because your time away from your desk and your bed is being used in the best kind of way.

HOW TO *ACTUALLY* SAY NO

Here's the thing. There is a high percentage of us who would identify as a 'people pleaser'. You don't like to upset the apple cart and take joy in other people's happiness and that's lovely. I would 100% put myself in that camp. If someone labelled me as an a-hole for my actions in some way then I would be mortified. Like 'Nip-slip at the Super Bowl' mortified. For others that might not be as much of an issue and in which case please feel free to sprinkle some of your 'IDGAF' attitude my way, but for those of us who like to please, saying 'no' can feel gut-wrenching.

You know what's worse than declining an invite though? Declining an invite when you've previously said yes. Ahhhh – *a flake*. No one likes a flake. No one wants to be a flake. It's a much nicer experience for everyone involved – yourself included – if you're just honest about your non-attendance intention from the get-go. Here's how to address some potentially tricky situations if 'no' doesn't come all that naturally.

In the heat of the moment the easiest option is to nod and agree to social events that you don't much fancy. Now it's a bit of a lame get-out, but avoid confirming anything at the time and use the ol' '*I'll have to check my diary - it's not currently up to date*' line and respond at a later date excusing yourself.

This feeling is THE WORST. The 'I'm disappointed' line is one that we all dread receiving. But if you're really not feeling it then be honest. It might help your friend understand better if you explain your reasons for declining and maybe you can manoeuvre the occasion into something that suits you both.

Ahhh repaying favour debt - the classic. If you feel uneasy about the amount of work you're putting in, speak up. Maybe there's something else they can do to scratch your back, or perhaps you can scale back on the tasks that you owe? If you're struggling to find a way to incorporate it into your schedule, be honest and acknowledge that you're aware of your favour-owing situation and ask if there's any wiggle room with the dates.

Sometimes you might feel like going through with an event because ultimately it's for a good cause or you're really helping someone out, but deep down you know you just can't fit it in. Maybe there's a way you can support from the sidelines? Decline, but send encouragement and ask for any other ways you can be involved.

You live and you learn and through experiencing these scenarios you'll fine tune your yes/no switch to be a fully sharpened tool that hopefully results in finding some kind of harmony in your life, work and home schedules and allows more time to do the stuff that puts a whopping great grin on your face. No flakes to find here.

The Edit

With such a big emphasis on having an absolutely banging Instagram-worthy social life that includes multiple holidays a year with your mates to exotic locations, weekly dinners out and sparklers in bottles of alcohol that cost more than you'd ever wish to spend on a pair of shoes, it's no wonder that we feel pressure to up the ante with our free time. If that makes you happy and you have a soft spot for pyrotechnics and Grey Goose, then be my guest. If it doesn't, then it's not something that you should feel shit about. Your social life is there to inject joy back into the sometimes mundane throes of life, and with the confidence to say no, thanks to the methods outlined above, hopefully you're feeling more optimistic about slicing up your non-working hours so they serve you best. Plus you have some new ideas of how to spice up your next mate date. Did someone say 'disco party, glow-in-the-dark fancy dress vegan aerial yoga'?

Our social lives revolve around short-term plans – the birthdays, the lunch breaks, the weekly Pilates/gossip session – but what about when we want to start thinking further ahead? How do we incorporate everything we've covered so far into an edited life plan that catapults us to the place where we want to be five years down the line? Don't worry, I have just the ticket...

Creating goals and your future plans

Learn how to structure long-term goals into everyday life to add purpose and direction, so that you actually see them through and know what to do when it doesn't all go to plan.

Having been part of my secondary school netball team in the position of goal shooter, I know a thing or two about goals. Not only is it a great feeling when you score one, it takes strategy and practice to be in with a chance of achieving one. I can also recommend playing the part of goal shooter in netball if you enjoy chatting and minimal running in sports. It was my ideal position. Despite making the measly C team during our primary school try-outs, I tried my go again at making the top tier when I graduated to senior school, and thanks to my long arms and even longer legs which made me about a foot taller than any of my teammates (yes, I did look like Stretch Armstrong), I finally made the A team. I surprised myself by not being completely awful. I often made friends with the goalkeeper from the other team – especially if their teammates were absolutely obliterating us – and scored a fair number of goals. Of course, this wasn't a coincidence. We practised every week, come rain or shine, with the dream of winning the yearly county tournament. We had a purpose and we did everything we could to achieve it, including turning into human ice blocks on the court, wearing skirts without joggers underneath because we thought it made us look the part. Sadly, we never got to lift that trophy, but we did come fourth one year – HOORAY! – and it taught me a valuable lesson about focus, determination, the importance of goal setting, and also that pleated skirts just weren't a good look for me.

A goal can mean a swish of a ball through a hoop, or kicking a ball to hit the back of a net, but in the context of an edited life, a goal is an ending to strive towards. It's a direct result of your ambition. A mission statement crafted by you that you wish to realise for your personal, physical, financial or mental gain. It might be a small tweak, like vowing to drink two litres of water every day. I know, I'm *so* original. It seems like a little adjustment, but ultimately you're aiming to be more hydrated and reap all the benefits that come with it – COME AT ME DEWY SKIN. Or perhaps you're shooting for the stars and want to put yourself through further education in order to secure yourself your dream job at the end of it. YAS GIRL! They don't have to be small, or big, but creating personal goals for yourself hands you a framework that, when deployed, steers your life in the direction you want it to head in.

If you *really* get down to the nitty gritty, without goals we're goal-*less*, which basically equates to directionless. I mean, it sounds dramatic, but a fire in our bellies for at least *something* gives us purpose and an outcome to aim towards. When you break it down, goals actually provide us with our daily to-dos, which act as incremental building blocks that lay together in order to form the big picture, and eventually we get there – whether it takes a week or a year, or five.

Your goals might be sitting there already, just quietly minding their own business, but moulding your attitudes and decision making without you really tapping into their true source, or maybe you're an avid goal setter who has them pinned up to your fridge so you can see them every morning when you manage to roll out of bed. Whichever one of those situations you relate to – or even if you're somewhere in between – this chapter is going to show you how to create your own goals in the first place and subsequently how to edit them in as part of your everyday life. It's time to hit the back of the net.

You've reached the final chapter in the *Life* section of this book, so you have most of the foundations for an edited life laid already. You've cleaned out your calendar, got to grips with your personal budget, are hopefully nourishing yourself with good food, fitness and some well-deserved sleep, and you're trying to carve more time out of your schedule for you to use however you wish. You're ticking the boxes. So where do you go from here? Well, in terms of moving forward and looking into your Mystic Meg crystal ball at the future, it's time for you to dig deep and work out what the hell it is that you want, aside from Ryan Gosling arriving at your door holding two fluffy kittens.

At the beginning of this book I said that homework wasn't really my style, but this is one of a few steps that benefits from grabbing a pen and a piece of paper and having a heart-to-heart with yourself. So, here's my step-by-step for a goal-setting session – it's a good place to start:

1 Imagine Ryan Gosling shouting at you 'WHAT DO YOU WANT?' – you know, like he does at Rachel McAdams in *The Notebook*? He actually says: 'Stop thinking about what I want, what he wants, what your parents want. What do *you* want?', which is exactly the point here. Thanks for that, Ryan.

2 Split your page into four and head each section with one of the following topics: **financial**, **wellbeing**, **personal** and **career**. Of course if there are other headings that fit better with your potential goals, then be my guest. I find that creating these sections allows you to whip out the magnifying glass on one particular area of your life, to work through it with a fine-tooth comb.

3 Is there anything that jumps to the forefront that you'd like to conquer? What do you feel like you're conquering already? Is there anything you'd like to advance in, or improve on? You might find that you're stumped in some sections, but can't stop writing goals down for others. There ain't no rules here! Scribble away and when you're done, you'll have your answers for Ryan nailed.

In case you need some ideas, here are my current goals:

FINANCIAL

- Put away at least £250 a month to save for costs and fees for the next time we move.
- Avoid buying a designer bag for the next 12 months and enjoy using what I currently own.

WELLBEING

- Drink two litres of water (at least!) every single day.
- Give four new fitness classes a try over the next 12 months.

PERSONAL

- Aim to get my mobile phone screen time to under two hours a day.
- Be better at replying to messages and just generally be a better friend.
- Read one book a month.

- Learn the skills to operate photo editing software like Light Room or Photoshop.
- Get a piece of my writing published in a magazine.

So you've got some personal goals down on paper? FAB. Ryan is going to be so impressed! Maybe you feel like there are some that will require some serious work (aka *no fancy bags for the rest of the year* – ha!), or perhaps you feel like they'll be a stretch, but they're achievable in a pretty short space of time. Whatever the goal and no matter the timeframe, you've got the roots of your motivation firmly planted, and these will act as a guide for all planning, scheduling and productivity decisions you make in the future – even if you don't realise it at the time. But before we get to the next step, it is important to look at each of these goals and work out where they sit on the specificity scale. Take 'drink two litres of water a day', for example – it's simple and clear, and you'll be able to track when you've reached your goal. However, something like 'be a better friend' is a tad more vague. How do you measure that? And how do you put it into practice? Before you go any further, highlight the ones that might need a little more help to transform themselves into shiny action points, and then it's time to polish them up.

How to set goals you'll actually score

Before you get down to business, here are the four steps to run each of your goals through that will transform each one into action points you'll be sure to tick off eventually. Less dilly-dallying, more doing.

MAKE THEM S.M.A.R.T.

Fine-tuning your goals to be S.M.A.R.T. is a guaranteed way to iron out any niggles and karate chop away any obstacles that might crop up down the road. You're looking to make your goals:

Specific
Measurable
Achievable
Realistic
Time-managed

So take the end goal of '*I want to get fit*'. It's a good idea, but it might be one that you've promised yourself you'll get round to for the past three years, and the only thing you've done is Google local gyms and then got distracted by the advert for leggings that came up on the side. In fairness I'm sure those leggings are great for watching TV in, too. So in order to make it a goal you actually get your teeth into, it's time to inject the S.M.A.R.T. antidote.

How about instead saying 'I will attend two workout classes at the gym per week, for the next three months'? Firstly, it's **specific** – there's no arguing with that. It's also **measurable** because you can tick off your two sessions per week as you go. Twice a week is certainly something that could fit in with your schedule without too much re-jigging and it's **achievable** given your current fitness levels. 12 weeks doesn't feel like an eternity, but it's also long enough to give a new habit a go and see some changes, so being stamped with that time period seems like a **realistic, time-managed** idea. *See?* It makes sense. Doing this across all your goals will leave you with action points to implement, like, now.

I know it sounds a little '*wheatgrass shot sipping, while wearing linen loungewear and lapping up your beach-view from your kitchen*', images I promised this book would never conjure up, but there is something about having your goals visible in a high-traffic spot that, for me anyway, keeps them at the forefront of my mind and therefore more likely to actually happen. I used to set goals at the beginning of every year – *yep, that ol' chestnut* – and by about 10th February if you had questioned me on what they were, I probably wouldn't have been able to give you an accurate answer. Which defeats the whole point of setting them in the first place and proves that I was mustering up lacklustre goals that I didn't feel strongly enough about. However, the one year that I typed them up, printed them out and kept them as a reminder for the whole 12 months, pinned up over my desk and next to my computer, I ended up ticking about six out of eight off the list. Coincidence? I think not.

It's human nature that when we restrict something and tell ourselves that we're not allowed it, we want it even more. Case in point: whenever I begin a healthy eating kick after ordering way too many Domino's the week before, it's always approximately 48 hours before I'm raiding the freezer to find the tub of Ben & Jerry's Phish Food that I KNOW is in there somewhere. It's the main reason why I avoid diets and food restrictions like the plague, keep my food intake rule-

free and aim for the 'everything in moderation' approach instead.
ICE CREAM AND PIZZA FOR ALL (and veggies and fruit too). So
instead of a goal that focuses on avoidance – like 'I will not eat any
sugary snacks' – try to frame it in a way that focuses on inclusion: 'I
will aim to eat at least five servings of fruit and veg every day.' This
way your brain is tricked into thinking about nourishing foods and your
willpower remains poised and intact (and the Ben & Jerry's remains in
the freezer).

ME, MYSELF AND I

Goal setting in this way is a solitary activity. It's personalised to
you, and although it might be handy to use others as a soundboard,
remember to spin back to Ryan's advice and think only about your own
expectations and ambitions for yourself. Let me tell you I don't think
self-employed blogger would have been on the cards for my parents'
wishes for me, but I couldn't be happier in my career. Plus my dad has
been one of my biggest supporters and assists me with the financial
side of my business – THANKS DAD – and my mum enjoys all the
hand cream PR freebies that come her way. Straying off the path that
my psychology degree was sending me on thanks to the expectations
of others, my grades and encouragement from my teachers, was a lucky
break that surprised those around me; I didn't realise at the time that
it was one of the riskiest moves I've made, but one that has thankfully
paid off. So shut down the voices in your head that aren't yours and
focus on your own that might be whispering away in the corner. Also,
aim to set goals that require you, and you only, in order to succeed.

Right, your goals are ripe and ready, and slapped up in a place where
you can see them every single day? FAB. Now it's time to incorporate
them into your life in a way that feels effortless and so that you can
track them to keep an eye on their progress too. In order to do that we
firstly need to come up with an action plan for each one. Now it doesn't
need to be formulated into a bloomin' chart like I have opposite (yes
I know I'm a teacher's pet), but just have a think about what you're
going to need to do on a daily, weekly and monthly basis in order to get
to the finish line. The chances are that the daily to-dos are behaviours
that will become habits after time (plus you'll have the daily reminder
thanks to your visible goals wherever you've got them on show), but
the weekly and monthly pointers might be something that you can add
into your diary to give them a sense of importance, and so you actually
complete them. Here are three of my current goals broken down:

	DAILY	WEEKLY	MONTHLY
Save at least £250 a month into a savings account.	Avoid mindless spending on food and clothing when out and about and stick to budget.	Update my budget weekly to make sure that I'm on track with my spending.	Set up a direct debit so money is automatically deposited into savings, and top up if possible.
Get my mobile screen time to under 2 hours a day.	Download the Moment app to track on-screen time. Check the results the following morning.	Analyse the data in the Moment app for the past week, notice patterns and alter my habits as required.	Complete one digital detox to further break the phone/palm bond.
Give 4 new fitness classes a try over the next year.	Keep an eye out for fitness classes that I fancy giving a go, and recommendations from friends and family.	Keep up with my fitness routine and feel out what sort of workout I'd like to try next. Research ideas.	Narrow the choices down and every 3–4 months book a new fitness class in.

The daily to-dos are behaviours that I'll eventually click into; adding weekly and monthly reminders into my iCal, to actually do the tasks that I've set out above, and suddenly I have goals that I'm actively working towards 24/7 in a way that doesn't feel overwhelming – and in a way where I actually have a decent chance of seeing them through. I'd suggest doing the same in your calendar – highlighting action points in your paper diary, or setting up recurring reminders digitally – or if you're more of a Bullet Journal kinda gal, setting up a double-page spread with your goals and the daily, weekly and monthly action plans on one side, with a dated checklist to tick off on the other.

Some goals might be completed in a week, others in a month. However, the most common stretch of time that we give ourselves is 12 months. Let's have a chat about resolution furore: is it worth it?

A WORD ON NEW YEAR'S RESOLUTIONS

You might have noticed throughout this chapter that I've peppered in the odd reference to *12-month* periods, which coincidently is a year, which not so coincidentally brings us to the topic of New Year's Resolutions. They're a bit like Marmite, aren't they? Some people love 'em and lap them up every single year come 1st January, and others can't stand the thought of them and head to Twitter to express their distaste for the 'New Year, New Me' concept. Personally, I fall into the former category. I'm a big fan of setting goals and the first day of the first month of the year makes me feel like I have a fresh page in the book. I'm a sucker for the first day of anything. The first day of school, the first day of a new job – give me an excuse to buy a pencil case, organise my belongings and have the ability to feel brand new, and I'm IN. It's the only other time of year, aside from the beginning of September, where there's that 'new school year' vibe hanging in the air, and I get it. It's catching.

If you like the idea and the time is right, then go ahead. Set yourself some goals, use the tips I've shared above and be on your merry way. If that doesn't sound like your bag, then hear me out. Where I feel like we often go wrong with the idea of resolutions is that we feel that if we haven't set them on 1st January then we've missed our chance and we must wait another 363 days till we can even think about goal setting again. WRONG. Sure, they might then not fall into the category of 'New Year's Resolutions', but if you find yourself itching to set some goals for yourself in August that you'd like to have completed by December, or maybe even the following summer, then what's stopping you? Stick two fingers up at the classical framework and get your goal-setting started whenever you feel is right.

Throughout the years, I've had varying amounts of success with my resolutions. Some years I've stuck to some for the allotted time. The almost-two-year dalliance I had with weight-lifting at the gym from 2015–2017 was a highlight. However, some years it gets to just two weeks after I've set them and I've yet to make any progress, so I rip out the page in my notebook and forget about resolutions until the next New Year's Eve rolls around. Case in point: my inability to ever stick with the resolution to go to language classes to brush up on my French and Italian (probably due to my crippling fear of speaking aloud in a foreign language, which is exactly why I should give one-on-one tuition a go before I head to class) or the resolution to wear proper clothes every day and get dressed in the morning as though I was going to an office so I feel more 'prepared' (why wear a rigid waistband if you don't have to, eh?). What I've found works best for me is to keep my goals at the forefront of my mind, whether that's pinning them up like I do above my desk, or creating a moodboard if visuals are more your thing, and actually taking the time to curate them in the first place. Instead of creating goals that align with the same ones my friend has set, or just because having a smoothie for breakfast is all the rage these days, actually thinking about me. What motivates me, what I enjoy and what I want to be better at on a daily basis.

Another common error is that we mistake our resolutions for being rigid and unmoving. But what if we're a quarter of the way through the year and we've set ourselves the task of learning a new musical instrument and we absolutely HATE IT? The idea of ukulele practice makes you want to send in a sick note from your mum to excuse your attendance? If you've given your resolution a good crack and it's just not working for you, then re-think, re-jig and spend time working towards something that you actually enjoy putting the legwork into. Perhaps you just need to change teacher, or instrument, or you could try teaching yourself with the helpful hand of YouTube tutorials. Or maybe you're just not the next Jack Johnson. Remember to check in with your resolutions periodically – I'd suggest every three months as a minimum – and edit your goals as you see fit. Flexibility isn't a sign of failure or flakiness, but instead a sign of your ability to successfully reflect and recalibrate.

The elusive 'five-year plan'

New Year's Resolutions are something that we're all familiar with. There's a high percentage of the general public who get on board with them yearly, and if not, most have tried the concept on for size before. In the realm of goal setting, New Year's Resolutions are goals with a year-long time constraint. They tend to be on the smaller scale and part of a bigger slice of pie that we're aiming to bake up. So, what if you want to see how a five-year plan fits for you? See? We're talking *long term* now. Deep down somewhere, once you scrape past the layers of dewy foundations, fake tan and black clothing, we've probably all got a five-year plan cooking away and just bubbling along that we might not have tasted yet. They are some of the longest-term goals that we can set ourselves, and whether we're aware of them or not, they underpin pretty much everything we do.

Five-year plans are a topic that I get asked about frequently, probably because when you do a search online for information you're met with film-length YouTube videos and posts that would take you about four hours to read. The process is framed as being long and soul-searching, and on the surface it appears that you might indeed need five years just to think up your five-year plan. If I'm honest, the concept just isn't for me right now. Within a five-year window I went from living in the single box room of my parents' house and working full time with a four-hour round-trip commute, to being a homeowner and blogger who'd taken her hobby into a full-time job and couldn't quite believe it. In that space of time my goals were constantly shifting and changing, and I still find myself in that phase right now, where the end marker gets stamped back into the ground a foot on from where it had previously been the month before. Sure, the goals that might take me five years or more to complete are there and present deep down, but I feel like it would be too much on my plate currently to spew them out and have to concern myself with constantly readdressing them. Instead I'm happy with my goal setting over a year-ish period that doesn't feel overwhelming and seems to be working for me right now. I am two years into attending regular reformer Pilates sessions and I won't shut up about it. NEW YEAR'S RESOLUTIONS FTW.

However, I have friends who *have* found this five-year plan technique works for them, so I've picked their brains on how and why it jived better than a shorter-term plan. The overriding consensus is that they feel like it gives them a stronger sense of direction, and having this plan in their back pocket gives them a feeling of control over their lives when sometimes it feels like that isn't the case. Most used it to put some meat on the bones of career goals, whereas others focused more on all aspects of where they'd like their life to be in five years' time, and what they'd like to do between now and then. One thing they all agreed on was that it gives them the ability to add headlines onto each year. So, for example, one year might be a year of saving, the next a year of travel, followed by a year of working up the career ladder. This means that they are able to point their goals each year in the direction of the year's title and give themselves a better chance of ticking them off. So your five-year plan trickles down into yearly goals, which can be chopped into mini New Year's Resolutions, *kinda*. It sounds appealing, right? Want to see if it's right for you?

Have you had success
at goal setting before?

When thinking
about your goals, do
you find the process
flows easily for you?

Were those past
goals that you set
yourself S.M.A.R.T.?

Do your goals lend
themselves to a
period longer than
12 months?

Does the idea of a
five-year plan feel
stressful or too
rigid for you?

Give a five-year
plan a go!

Stick to shorter-
term goals or New
Year's Resolutions

In terms of how they cobbled their own *long*-term goals together, no one's process made me wish that there was some magical 'eject me from my seat and send me to the moon' button, because it sounded so complicated; in fact, they were just as simple as cogitating a New Year's Resolution (*almost*). The key is to think of the end goal and work back from there. DUR. The goals are hefty – usually those relating to work and lifestyle – and often not that specific, like taking care of their physical and mental health, but every five-year goal can be broken down into smaller ones that slot in nicely with the S.M.A.R.T. method. I've taken their notes and made an easy-to-follow-without-wanting-to-fall-asleep four-step plan for creating your very own five-year plan. *Which isn't as catchy as it could be, I know...*

1 THINK ABOUT THE THREE WS Close your eyes, sit back and imagine where you want your life to be in five years' time.

Who are you? Of course you're still you unless modern medicine takes a real leap sometime soon, but we all change and remould over the years, so have a think about your lifestyle, daily habits, personal development – you know the stuff we all roll our eyes at but that is pretty important? Yeah, that.

Where are you? Perhaps you imagine yourself living within the same four walls, or would you like to move? Maybe it's down the road, maybe it's abroad?

What are you doing? Basically, what would you like to spend 40+ hours a week putting your time into in an ideal world? Aside from being an ice-cream taster, which has been my dream job since the age of three.

2 TURN 'EM INTO GOALS Once you've got the who, where and what in your mind, the end goals should become apparent, be it career, financial, personal or otherwise. You shouldn't have to dig too deep for them and if you are knee-deep with a trowel in your hand then it might be time to question why they're hidden so damn far underground.

Perhaps the answer to your 'where' query was that in five years' time you picture yourself doing the daily commute in the Big Apple. So one of your goals is that you'd like to live and find work in New York. TA-DAH. Untangle your answers and dust off those diamonds in the rough. All my friends suggest that five is the maximum to put your mind to here, so stick to that or less, to keep some spare storage on your brain-space hard drive.

A goal to live in N.Y.C. might seem like a far-out idea, but once you break it down into five year-long periods, it seems doable. That's the trick with this five-year plan schtick, it makes pretty much everything seem doable, and that's a cool tool to know how to use. So, for the example I've given here:

YEAR ONE: Adjust your budget, increasing your savings and taking up any additional income streams.

YEAR TWO: Build on this by increasing your savings account even more: sell old clothing online, do a car boot sale of your stuff from the loft, look for ways to sell your furniture when you eventually leave the country. Aim to double your savings from the year before, if not more.

YEAR THREE: Research into finding jobs, looking into the logistics of moving, paperwork and working visas.

YEAR FOUR: Secure things in place: find accommodation and interview for jobs or internships. Book flights and prepare yourself with a budget for when you move, so you won't end up dipping into debt once you get there.

YEAR FIVE: Move! Head to New York with all your belongings, move into your new home, start your new job and live the SATC dream. It might not take this long, or it might take longer, but this framework allows for flexibility and gives us the time to get shit done. Just celebrate with a Manhattan (or two!) when the plan works out.

4 FOCUS ON THE YEAR AHEAD. Ok, imagine the set-up here. Say you've given yourself three goals to achieve over a five-year period. You've broken them down further into five mini-goals to hit each year. All of a sudden you've got 15 goals laid out in front of you. *Now breathe.* My friends stressed the importance of this one to me, that at any one time just focus on the goal that's applicable for the year you're in. Don't try to skip ahead; get your head down and work your way through what you've set yourself to focus on right now. That way, whatever you're working towards feels achievable, instead of daunting. Just as you would a short-term goal or a New Year's Resolution, look at how they break down into daily, weekly and monthly habits and add key deadlines or check-ins into your calendar and schedule where possible. *Five years will fly by.*

Of course, life likes to cough up the odd obstacle here and there that can throw our goals off the scent. Sometimes they're annoying, but small and insignificant, potholes. Other times they're life-altering road blocks which might change the direction of your goals entirely. So how do we dust ourselves off and get back onto the proverbial ambition-filled horse when we've been bucked off?

Managing set-backs, because sometimes life ain't peachy

Have you been slapped across the face with life in a way that's made you stumble sideways and dizzy by the whole experience? WELL THAT SUCKS. Sending all my love and some advice your way…

- Cry. Then cry some more. Cry in public. Cry in the toilets at work. Cry under your sunglasses on the commute home. Cry at the TV. Cry because you've missed the start of *The Great British Bake Off*. I'm a big believer in crying. Especially the 'Ugly Cry' Kim Kardashian-style. It's therapeutic and holding it in and consequently burning the back of your throat is such an awful feeling. Let. It. Out.

Talk about it out loud if you feel like that might be useful. Ask for help and don't feel ashamed for doing so. Call up your best mate and chew her ear off on the phone. Have your friends over for takeaway and let them in on what's going on. Ask your mum, dad, sister, brother, extremely wise grandparent for advice. Kick the worry of burdening others to the back of your mind. You'd be just as dutiful if the same was asked of you in return.

Lean in to whatever feels right for you at the moment. Just been dumped and fancy signing up to Tinder now? I'll be more than happy to provide feedback on your chosen profile photo. Something shitty going on at work and you just can't bear the thought of keeping up with your gym routine tonight? That's fine, there's always next week. Been dealt a life event that you didn't see coming and just want to be on your own? No worries at all, cancel all socials in your diary and don't feel selfish about it. Listen to yourself and honour your answers.

Do you think some time away and out of your usual routine might make you feel better and help you gain some clarity on the situation? Book yourself a weekend away with friends on a city break. Or get a couple of days off work and go and stay with a mate on their sofa. I LOVE it when people come and stay on my sofa, and go all-out as though I'm running a five-star B&B. Hopefully your pals will feel the same. Visit your parents for the evening. A change of scenery, even for a short period of time, can work wonders.

Need to cry again? Go for it. Keep some dampened cotton pads in a sandwich bag in the fridge and thank me later for this de-puffing miracle.

You'll notice that all these situations are immediate. That's because all you really have to do is just to get through the day. Don't worry about tomorrow, or next week. Just focus on the 24 hours ahead of you. Fancy doing a combination of crying and drive-thru trips? FAB. Want to get stuck in with a big project to take your mind off it? BRILLIANT. Don't want to leave your bed and just want to watch nineties chick-flick classics while still in your pyjamas? I'M JOINING YOU.

Once you're done crying, being comforted and have watched *10 Things I Hate About You* for the 24th time, you might feel ready to readdress your goals. Perhaps the set-back has shifted them a little, or a lot. Maybe you want to scrap the whole thing completely, and that's cool. If there is no longer a fire in your belly that flickers at the thought of that end result, then ditch it. It's no big failure to admit that your heart isn't in something anymore. Let's stop being such a hardass on ourselves. Sometimes we need to quit and pull the plug on an idea. Sometimes we need to walk away. Sometimes we change, and with that the goalposts move too. There's always a new goal out there which will stoke the fire and get you motivated again. You might just need to view it differently or adjust your approach, but a set-back doesn't have to stop you from scoring.

The Edit

I'm well aware that this section could have been just 11 words long – *write down some goals and actually stick to them this time* – but we're all so bloody terrible at that so I thought it needed unpicking in detail. We're awful at it because we set unrealistic goals that don't excite us, that we set anyway because we feel like it's what we should be doing. It's a recipe for disaster that ultimately makes us feel shit and demotivated, because we feel like we're always failing, rarely ever seeing things through to the end.

But that's all about to stop, right? Now you know the rules to apply to make them doable. You're going to be S.M.A.R.T.- er about it. *You like what I did there?* You know the way to structure your future goals and the different timeframes you can try. Maybe you'll still be doing your New Year's Resolution come December, or maybe you'd like to try your hand at a longer-term five-year plan. Perhaps you just fancy working on your goal-setting muscle for now and want to give yourself one to tackle over the next month. You know that if it feels like a struggle – like putting on jeans after Christmas – to switch it out for something that fits better. Don't be afraid of moulding the end goal, or the journey you plan on taking to reach it.

Hopefully we're on the same page when it comes to the importance of goals. You might feel like you're sorted on the goal front, but giving up just the teeny tiniest amount of time to this section will really help you to lay your shit out on the table and work out how you'd like the pieces to fit together. Having this knowledge will not only help to wrap up everything else I've discussed so far with a big fat bow, but also becomes so important once we start to tackle the next section. You're learning to edit your life; well, now it's time to do the same to the world of work...

AN
EDITED
LIFE

CHECK
LIST

- [ ] Clear up your calendar and find a method that works best for you and your life. Add in all important dates, meetings and deadlines.

- [ ] Begin work on a budget. Start by tracking all your income and outgoings with the view to having a firm budget set up in six months' time.

- [ ] START BEING NICE TO YOURSELF! You know, like how you would be if you had a mate who had just been dumped. Rest when you need it, nourish yourself well and move every day. Plan out your dinners for the week ahead and get an early night.

- [ ] Do a digital detox and try not to throw your phone in the sea when it's over (there's a high possibility you may want to). Participate in them regularly.

- [ ] Say no to the next occasion that comes up that you really, *really* want to say no to. It's freeing and is the key to finding peace and happiness in your schedule.

- [ ] Switch off the noise for 15 minutes and have a think about what goals you'd like to make for yourself. Pin 'em up, look at them daily and use them as your motivation to kick ASS.

WORK

Now it's time to address the task that most of us spend 40 hours plus a week tackling – *work*. Careers get a bad rap. In the modern world we're depicted as a generation obsessed with them, often driven to the brink of burnout by just how much of our lives we dedicate to them and the pressures we feel our roles put us under. Now, I'm not proposing that work is supposed to be a completely stress-free environment – we're all going to feel the heat from time to time – but I do feel that there are a handful of methods we could all incorporate easily into our jobs that will give us some breathing space.

Spring-clean your desk because, just like my personal mantra, '*No good work gets done in jeans*', then '*No good work gets done on a desk where you can't even see the surface*'.

Let's see how we can turn the pressure notch down a little by structuring your time in the most effective way for you. Learn how to become an email PRO by setting yourself some ground rules and incorporating automation to your inbox.

Procrastination is a demon that's easily crushed, so let's stamp it out and set those motivation levels to an all-time high.

It's time to start getting shit done, in a way that doesn't make you feel so darn knackered all the time, and instead leaves you feeling satisfied and satiated with your work output...

Organise your workspace

By stripping back your desk-side clutter and creating a space free from distractions, planning your time and getting stuff done in the work place gets a whole lot easier. Promise.

You know the saying: tidy house, tidy mind. The same goes for your desk. A clear and organised workspace equals less visual clutter and distractions, which in turn allows for more brain space to get on with your work. It's hardly a groundbreaking notion, but it's one that sometimes gets forgotten as the paperwork mountains begin to rise and form over desks across the globe. Some jobs require a physical paper trail that's hard to keep on top of, whereas others might be more digital-focused, and it's less of a paper tower that you're creating and more of a Pret A Manger porridge pot one. Some of us might have no designated desk space in our roles, others might have their own office (check you out!). Maybe you've got your own cubicle, or you hot-desk, or perhaps you make up the 'work from home and only see the postman during your working day' contingent (that's me!).

However your job is set up, the chances are that you'll have some kind of workspace, and in order to instil some good basic habits into your work routine and Monday-to-Friday grind, it's a good idea to start with sorting your space so that it's set up in the most practical way for you and your role, with minimal distractions so you can ward off your mid-afternoon YouTube rabbit hole. This is the key to having an edited, organised working life.

My career journey has spanned all kinds of roles and workplaces. I began in retail (no desk space, just a locker to keep my mid-morning cookie stash in), then moved on to bar work (no space to call your own except a spot by the dishwasher to throw your bag down), finally ending up in a series of PR office jobs where I got to have my own desk and felt like a fully fledged adult. I did all the clichés: the potted plant, the mini photo frame, books, a spare jacket on the back of the seat – I practically moved in. The only thing I was missing was an American sitcom-esque cardboard box to collect all my belongings in when I left. When that moment did happen and I left my last PR role to go full time on the blog, I downgraded from a desk that was big enough for a four-person dinner party to a wonky laptop table from IKEA that *just about* fitted my laptop and was located next to the kitchen bin. It was an adjustment, for sure, but thanks to a pretty comfy chair, a vase of flowers that I refreshed weekly and stripping back my desk-side supplies to just the essentials, I ended up doing some of my best work in that kitchen nook.

These days I've upgraded to a home office. A WHOLE ROOM! I still can't get over it. I have a proper adult-sized desk and a printer! A sofa for if I feel like writing a blog post while lying down! A drawer to hide my secret post-it addiction! My set-up is considerably more roomy and practical these days, but in all honesty the work output is the same and that's the moral of the story here. It doesn't matter how big or small the spot you work in is, and it's nothing to do with how expensive or swishy the chair you're sitting on is, or how many people you could fit around your desk if you were to hold some weird dinner party/Christmas do mash-up. What's important is that your workspace is clear and tidy, easy to navigate, functional but comfy (especially if you have to sit there for long stretches of time) and leans in to whatever environment you feel most productive in. When life gives you a desk that barely fits a laptop and is generally unpleasant (especially if fish was on the menu the night before), you make sure it's organised and neat, source yourself an aesthetically pleasing pot plant to make the whole thing a little more pleasant, and get on with it. Whether you're in a cubicle or a café, a spot that's comfortable, calm and quiet is all you need. Is your space feeling more cramped and chaotic than you'd like it to be? Here's how to detox your desk:

THE ONE-HOUR DESK SPRING CLEAN ROUTINE

1 CLEAR YOUR DESK. You'll notice when we get to the 'get rid of all your shit' chapter in the next stage of the book, that I'm a big fan of making one gigantic pile at the beginning of a clear-out session. Get it out. Toss it into a heap and let the clear-out commence. Your physical reaction to seeing all your desk belongings in one place will most probably be one of dismay, plus the act of

clearing your desk to be completely free of stuff means that you can actually give it a spring clean while you're at it. If you don't have a desk but perhaps a locker, or a laptop bag that you keep all work-related bumf in, then the same rule applies.

Organise your office clutter by sorting it into piles.

PAPERWORK. Place your paperwork into one of three piles: one that's junk and ready to be recycled, another for paperwork that you have to keep and can't be digitally stored for some reason (perhaps contracts that need to be signed or client files that must be stored manually), and a pile for paperwork that would be best suited to being scanned into your laptop in PDF format (basically everything else).

DECORATIVE STUFF (that you don't even like the look of!). Got any knick-knacks that are just making the joint look messy and aren't bringing you any joy to look at? Bin 'em immediately – screw the pile.

THINGS YOU ACTUALLY USE. Reserve this pile for things that you find yourself using often – at least once a week – that it makes sense to have within arm's reach.

THINGS YOU DON'T. Group together items that could be donated or handed off to fellow employees (things like reading material you no longer need or office supplies you never really use). The less stuff that's out on your desk, the less chance there is of your eyes wandering off task and onto a distraction.

Ready for a rule? Here's a *little tiny* one that's easy to abide by, doesn't make me sound like an absolute tyrant and will help keep your newly clean and organised desk in check. If it's an item that you use in some capacity every single working day, then it's allowed to be in close proximity – either tucked away or neatly displayed on your desk. If it's not something that you use every day, Monday to Friday, then it must be stored in some way. Test it out for a week or so. 90% of what you need should require you being able to locate it without your butt even leaving your chair. If there's anything that you're having to heave yourself up for and traipse to the other side of the room to retrieve, then re-jig and re-organise until you're at a place where the only reason you need to get up is to grab your mid-morning croissant, not because you need a pen.

4   SORT OUT STORAGE. I'm not normally a fan of sourcing storage before you know exactly what's going in it, as you tend to just fill it with shit for the sake of it, but you've done the groundwork here. From your final pile of things you use often, you might find that you need some storage solutions. Perhaps a set of drawers next to your desk will come in useful to keep those files you need to keep organised and easy to find. Or maybe a little stationery holder for your pens and paperclips? A pencil case! An accordion file! A paper tray! You get the gist here. Office clichés they might be, but they actually do come in handy for keeping a desk orderly and organised, and having these helping hands in place and giving all your items a proper home will lessen the chance of the Leaning Tower of Paper making a reappearance. Get what you can from the supply cupboard and make a shopping list for when you hit up Paperchase on your lunch break.

My desk essentials

BULLET JOURNAL

All the details are coming up in the next chapter; there you'll learn that it's not really a *classical* Bullet Journal, but that I just use some of the techniques to help me plan and schedule. I do have the actual hardcopy of the notebook that they sell (seriously, a dotted notebook will change your life). I travel everywhere with it as it holds all my editorial plans and daily to-do lists.

STATIONERY

Despite being an actual stationery nerd I only own a few items because I know that cute covered notebooks are my hoarding weak spot, so I try not to even seek them out in the first place. I keep a blue ballpoint pen out, along with a pair of scissors, a ruler (handy for organisation in the Bullet Journal), a pack of post-its, a pink and a yellow highlighter to decipher between different things in my journal, and that's it. See? Stationery streamlined? CHECK.

READING MATERIAL

I don't keep much physical reading material out on my desk because 80% of what I read comes from online these days. However, there's often some kind of self-help 'GO GIRL – YOU CAN DO THIS' book that I'm working through that I like to keep out on my desk. As I read through these I like to post-it the pages that I think I'll find helpful at some point. They probably break the 'must use every day' rule, but I do tend to have a flick through at least once a week to reference a point or to get advice on something I'm working on. I've tried to justify it, but I have to admit that it does tart my desk up somewhat, and that's the true reason. But hey – a small stack of books never hurt anyone.

PAPERWORK

Everything that I do workwise is stored online or up there *points to the sky but has no idea how it all works*. Rarely there might be a contract I have to sign physically or a form I need to fill out and so I keep those out on display slap-bang centre of my desk so that I'm more likely to complete them ASAP. More often than not, though, the only piece of paperwork on my desk is a rather large pile of those pesky 'Sorry you were out' Royal Mail cards.

BEAUTY STUFF

I know my origins as a beauty blogger might cause you to think that I have a whole drawer of touch-up-related makeup items, but let's face it, I work from home, only ever have social interactions with the postman and only wear makeup on the three-ish times a week that I actually see people who aren't the postie or my husband. Therefore the only beauty item that I keep out on my desk is a lip balm because that's really all I ever need to reach for throughout the day. If I did work in an office I think I'd beef it up with a concealer, eyebrow comb, face mist (because air con is a *beyatch*) and a lip colour to do that whole day-to-night thing.

I know we're talking about desk essentials here, but aside from my desk my home office spot includes a couple of other basics. I have a printer hidden as best as I can under my desk (try making a printer chic – it's impossible!), a padded office chair that swivels (a swivel chair is MUST, mostly just because it's fun) and a desk light which comes in extremely handy in the winter months when it gets dark at 3pm, plus makes nice mood lighting for when the office doubles up as a second bedroom for guests.

Seeing as the number of people who don't commute to your standard office setting is on the rise, along with flexible working arrangements, I thought I'd add in a little nod to those who work from home, either full time or on the odd occasion. Having worked in the offices of start-ups for over two years, I couldn't quite believe that shimmying around in my dressing gown constituted work. Who cared about the fact that I opened my laptop at 7am and closed it 12 hours later. I COULD DO WORK WITHOUT WEARING PROPER TROUSERS! Working from home and on your own is an odd thing. It's a world of elasticated waistbands, but no Christmas parties or work socials. A life of everyone thinking that you're available 24/7 and wanting to see you on their days off.

Let's just say I've had the Jeremy Kyle-watching, biscuit-eating, '*When was the last time I left the house?*' period and I was left feeling foggy and bloated and in desperate need of a shower. It wasn't cute, nor particularly motivating. No matter where we work, we're all going to have days where our bellies feel like we've eaten a melon whole and we just want to watch whatever bizarre topic Holly and Phil are covering and ignore our increasingly long to-do list – but the less of those we have, the better. After almost seven years of being part of the home-working population, here are my three golden rules:

Don't even *think* about switching on daytime TV. Step away from the remote.

Use your time at home to nourish yourself with proper food, not just multiple packets of biscuits. It's tempting and, let me tell you, I have eaten a pack of Bourbon biscuits for lunch many a time, but the best way to fix your habit is to make sure you don't buy the biscuits in the first place, and to fill your cupboards with nutrients galore. I'm a grazer, so instead make sure I have homemade snacks to eat during the day for my 11am snack, 2pm snack, 3pm snack and 4pm snack. I love snacks.

Leave the house every day. NO EXCUSES. Even if it's just a walk around the block. It really works wonders both mentally and physically and will help to unblock any creative arteries that are feeling clogged.

Make it work

So – working from home or an office, you're still working somewhere. Of course everyone's set-up is going to be different, but there are some fundamentals that will help you to dial in to your work flow whatever and wherever your setting. These tips can be shifted to make them applicable for you.

SAFETY FIRST

I know I sound like a boring health and safety Powerpoint presentation, but sitting comfortably is key. You know the whole diagram of the person sitting upright with their screen in their direct eye-line? It's spot on and our spines will thank us for it in years to come. So whatever you do and wherever you're sitting, just make sure you're comfortable, not cramping up and have some decent lumbar support going on. Plus, keep your screen brightness set to no more than about 75%.

AT HOME: Make sure that at least every hour, if not every 30 minutes, you're having a five-minute break from your laptop. I like to switch between tasks that require a laptop and those that don't, to avoid feeling like I haven't looked at anything that isn't a screen come bedtime.

AT THE OFFICE: You guys have the gift of regular meetings. YOU GET TO SEE OTHER PEOPLE! Use this time as a break from your screen and take notes with a pen and paper, if possible, to take advantage of getting away from the glare.

USE YOUR LUNCH BREAK WISELY

When I worked in retail, lunch breaks were golden because one, they were a break, and two, it meant that I could buy a slice of pizza from the van outside the shopping centre. These days lunch is something that we tend to bypass as quickly, due to our bulging to-do lists and a lack of time. Now, I'm not suggesting that you cook up a three-course meal, but it's something to be savoured, it's a 'break' – the clue is the name – and it's definitely not something to be consumed al-desko.

AT HOME: Step away from wherever it is that you're working, even if you just take yourself off your desk chair and plonk yourself in the armchair in the front room. A change of surroundings will help to break up the day. And resist the urge to eat something that's just pants and will leave you feeling hungry in half an hour anyway. Last night's leftovers? Perfect.

AT THE OFFICE: Again, remove yourself from your desk and take advantage of any staff break areas that are available to you. Resist the urge to check work emails while you eat, and if you do scroll as you chow down, use the time to catch up with friends and family, not industry chat. Bringing in your own lunch supplies is great for the ol' budget, but if you have the time then head out for 10 minutes, even if you don't need to grab lunch – to stretch your legs, get some vitamin D to your bones and fresh air in your lungs.

LISTEN TO YOUR BODY

Along with handing in your letter of resignation, calling in sick is one of the most heart-pounding things you can do at work; it just makes you feel like a let-down. But listen to your body. Pushing through a bout of flu or a sickness bug while also pushing through your to-do list means that you're not giving your body the time out it needs, and the work that you're completing will be nowhere close to your usual quality.

AT HOME: Taking a sick day when you work for yourself is a tough call, but tapping out for however long is needed for you to recover is an important realisation to come to terms with. We get sick, and when we do, we need to rest. So put away the laptop, be kind to yourself and do what your body is telling you that you need to do – switch off.

AT THE OFFICE: No one fancies sitting next to a bundle of germs from nine to five, so let your boss know ASAP that you're not feeling the ticket, and either take a sick day if you feel like death warmed up, or negotiate working from home if you feel like you're up to a day at work, but don't fancy infecting your fellow colleagues thanks to your every-10-minute sneeze fits. They'll thank you for it.

YOUR COLLEAGUE CREW

Colleagues are always a bit of a lottery. They're either fab '10 years after you both quit and you're still mates' material, or not. Either way you still have to work together, and trust me, if you work from home you'll even end up missing those who you'd time your trips to the staff kitchen against so as not to cross over. So respect them all, build relationships, and at the end of the day they are the only people in your life who know *exactly* what you're going through at work. You're in the same boat! So work on your sea legs and join the team.

AT HOME: The freelance life is pretty colleague-less unless you count your accountant and your clients. However, the chances are that there'll be people in your local town who are in a similar boat – so connect! Check on Facebook for local groups, or use apps like Bumble Bizz to connect and network. Build a crew where you can all support each other, give advice and hold a Christmas party so you're not left out of the world's worst hangover come 3rd December.

AT THE OFFICE: Feedback is a huge part of working in a team, and so when dishing it out, do so in a way that's calm and with evidence, and when receiving it, take it with dignity and apply it to change your course of action where needed. Just like with your friends, show

appreciation to your workmates when they've done you a favour;
everyone loves cake brought in for lunch or a notecard to say thanks.

E.O.D.

Whatever set-up you work in, the end of the day *needs* to be the end of
the day. In the modern world our working day is trickling into the hours
on either side of it, and often we find ourselves checking our inbox
when we wake up and replying to the final dregs in our inbox before
we fall asleep. WE NEED TO STOP! Unplugging from our roles
when we're off the clock is something that's healthy for us all to do.

AT HOME: If you can, keep your working day contained to one room,
as it gives you the option to close the door at the end of the day. If
that's not possible the next best thing is a dedicated spot in your home;
any nook you can fit a desk in or a corner of your kitchen table that you
could transform into a comfortable working space. Pack it away at the
end of the day to avoid the temptation to answer just *one more email*. If
neither of these ideas sounds appealing, then you could fence off all
your to-do list to be completed when you're out of the home, and set
up in local coffee shops or libraries, or join a co-working space where
you can usually hot-desk or pay for your own dedicated desk, for a
lower cost than renting your own office.

AT THE OFFICE: Traditionally, work is done at your desk, and then
when you're free to leave at the end of the day, you've clocked out.
However, that's not necessarily the case: I've seen how all my friends
now take work home with them. If there's a specific deadline or you're
feeling ridiculously snowed under and feel like one weekend of
hardcore work will ease your stress levels – I get it. However, try not to
make that the norm, by not bringing your work laptop home with you
at the weekends, switching your work phone off outside of working
hours (if possible) and using an O.O.O. (and abiding to it) whenever
you're away.

The Edit

So the real organisation shit has BEGUN! We'll get to the good stuff later in the book, so keep your bin bags on standby – but hopefully the act of detoxing your desk of unnecessary paperwork and clutter has got you in the mood. It's good to start with a small space and work your way up, and by putting in the time here first, you'll notice a difference immediately during your working day as you have fewer distractions in front of you and feel like you're ready to tackle your workload in the most efficient way. There'll be no more having to press pause for 15 minutes while you locate a lost document. I know the PDF conversions sound like an absolute faff, and yes, it might take an afternoon out of your schedule, but by dedicating hours to tasks that streamline your own processes you're only doing yourself a favour; Future You will be very thankful for the legwork you're putting in, I'm telling you.

You feel neat and organised, right? The physical mess has been cleared, so now it's time to apply the same processes to your working day and planning techniques. You'll learn how to clear the path and free up space so you can stick to deadlines without having to bury yourself away for two days before the work is due, to get it finished. We're tackling the big one as well – EMAILS. Your desk already looks like a Virgo's dream and soon your inbox will too...

How to plan your working day

It's time to nail time management and task scheduling, so your plans for the working day ahead are looking realistic, stress-free and edited in a way that best suits you, your role and your energy levels.

If I was going to pinpoint my particular edited life strengths, then time organisation would be right up there. Sure, I can budget, prep my meals, and who doesn't like a Sunday afternoon spent practising self-care – but planning my week? I'm just saying that if it was an Olympic sport, then ship me off to training camp pronto. It's one of the top tasks that makes me feel like I have my shit in order. Over the years I've refined my skills at chunking out my days in a way that gets my tasks completed, but that doesn't, when I look at it, leave me breathless like an old dog on a walk that's been a *little* too long. You've already tidied up your calendar, have got purpose underpinned by set goals, and are working out how to balance the self-care/socialising scales, so now let's tackle how best to incorporate your career into it and set out the hours of your working day.

There are two skills to hone here. First of all, it's all about slotting those tasks in. Perhaps your workload and structure of your day are dictated for you. You have a role where you know exactly what you need to do and when, and there isn't much budging in that. Fab. Some sections of the chapter ahead might not apply and others may be adapted to fit into aspects of planning for both your life and the home. However, others might find that, although the end goal and scope of the work is set out, the journey to actually getting there is all on you. The deadline is set, but the plan on how to achieve it is a little loose, so here's where the methods that I'm about to share with you really come into play.

Once you've nailed scheduling, it's about timekeeping in a way that works for you. How often do you get to the end of the week and feel like you've done nothing? Or that you haven't quite done enough? Well, a realistically structured plan can help with that, and when ticked off can act as a visual 'HELLO – LOOK AT WHAT YOU'VE DONE!' reminder. A well-laid plan that's been executed pretty much perfectly is about as satisfying as someone saying they're running late to a meeting when you're running late too. *Joyous*. But, you know, you're obviously going to be a *master* timekeeper by the end of this chapter. Yes, even you at the back whose mates tell you that the time you are meeting for dinner is an hour earlier than it actually is because you're a failsafe bet to rock up at dessert. Planning your time effectively will not only combat this 'dessert-time arrival' *thing*, but the addition of routine into your days will allow your goals from the previous chapter to be easily incorporated, and will give you a head-start on kicking procrastination in the arse, which we'll tackle next.

I haven't always been so successful at planning. I mean, don't get me wrong, I've always planned; I'm a child of the nineties, and let me tell you my padlocked fluffy notebook was chocker with organisation tit-bits, odes to boys who wouldn't go near me with a bargepole, and interior design plans for my room (I was very heavily influenced by *Changing Rooms* at the time – like I said, *child of the nineties*). But as I went through school, graduated into the world of work and then ended up working for myself, I actually over-planned my schedule. Over-planning is just as horrendous as failing to prepare, as it's basically like micro-managing yourself. Who wants a manager who breathes down your neck all day but IN YOUR BRAIN? Yeah, it sucks. I'd reserve a page a day in my notepad for my to-do list and then proceed to fill the whole thing. Instead of grouping a selection of smaller tasks together that when combined tick off a larger goal, I would write down every single minute detail. A task that would take me five minutes and could easily be incorporated into another item? Yeah, stick it on. My daily to-do lists were massive and it's no surprise that I never got to the end of them. EVER. I genuinely can't think of a time when I ticked off everything that I'd set myself to do in a day. I'd get two-thirds through the list of 25 or so items and feel like a complete and utter failure when I didn't reach the end. I'd stay up late. I'd get up early. I'd cut down my lunchtime to just 10 minutes and give myself a tasty episode of indigestion. But no matter what I did I was never in with a chance.

My lists were unrealistic, too detailed and ultimately made me feel pants because I never reached the finish line. I wasn't even close.

Then I learnt to edit. I wondered what would happen if I condensed the list down? Fewer items to tick off equals more chance of getting them done, was my thinking (SPOILER: it worked). Instead of breaking down all the steps that would have to happen in order for me to upload a video, I just wrote down 'upload and schedule video'. All of a sudden eight to-dos downsized into one, and even though the end result was exactly the same, it seemed less daunting and more manageable. Sometimes we have to play tricks on our minds, and often they fall for it. Overnight it looked like I had less on my plate even though I hadn't, and my plans didn't feel so stifling. Over the next couple of days I tweaked around tasks and played with wording, and before I knew it I'd got to the end of the day and comfortably worked my way through every single task. Instead of faffing around and getting bogged down with all the little things, I'd focused instead on three overriding tasks that I needed to get done – and I did 'em. Simple.

Record the video
Save the video into editing software
Edit the video
Export the video
Upload the video to YouTube
Fill out description box and title
Create and add a thumbnail to the video
Schedule the video and all social media posts

Upload and schedule video

So it took a while for me to find my time-management and planning sweet spot – both with work and with my social life – and the same might be true for you. Don't be afraid to completely switch up the methods you currently use and try something new. In doing so you might find yourself powering through your plans. What's to lose, eh?

An unproductive day or two? We all have those anyway! Possessing Beyoncé's work ethic 100% of the time isn't the most realistic goal, so let's aim for 80% instead. More days where you feel like you've been productive over feeling like you haven't even got started, is the end game here. Maybe it's the same story for you and you're a chronic over-planner who needs to simplify your tasks, or perhaps you find that beefing your to-do list out is a better motivator. I like to be quite regimented with my time (*what a surprise!*) and find I work best when I slot tasks into a certain day and have a rough plan of what order I'd like to complete them in. But I have some friends who plan tasks to get completed within a week and don't like to pin them down to particular days, and others who plan their days to the hour. THE HOUR! But hey, I'm not judging, because planning is such a personal thing, and that's why I'm going to present you with a handful of options that you can apply and edit in a way that suits you.

How to structure your day

STEP #1: TAP INTO YOUR ENERGY LEVELS

There is a factor that we all need to work into our planning processes, however we decide to structure our days, and that's our personal energy levels. I'm not going all '*chakras and auras*' on you. I'm talking about our energy and ability to focus and really get stuck in. We're not constantly at full power, not even Beyoncé. Instead we're on a scale that ebbs and flows during the day, week and month. For example, I'm a morning person who tends to get all my best work done before lunchtime. 3pm is a time for me when I can guarantee I'll be in some procrastination dark hole and then things pick up just before I pack up for the end of the day around the 5pm mark, where I can squeeze out my last bit of work. That's just me, it's how I work now and always have, and so now I plan my schedule accordingly.

Over the next working week track either in your notepad – or digitally if you find it easier – the times when you:

- Feel most energised and pumped about tackling those important tasks that demand brainpower.

- Feel brimming with creativity and full of inspiration.

- Are most likely to dive down an endless pit of 'Vocal Coach Reviews Lady Gaga's Best Performance' videos.

- Feel like cancelling on your mates/every plan you've ever made and have coming up, because the sofa just looks SO tempting.

Once you have your findings, use these timings to schedule tasks accordingly. So for me I follow these rules when it comes to planning my day:

MORNING (7AM-12PM)

Reserved for high-priority tasks that require the most brainpower, as this is when I'm at my most productive.

EARLY AFTERNOON (1PM-4PM)

I try to do more creative tasks that I find the most enjoyable, to attempt to hold my attention.

END OF THE DAY (4PM-6PM)

I answer emails and complete admin tasks, to make the most of that final surge of energy.

Know yourself, listen to your energy levels and tune in to where your head is at during certain times of the day. If possible, work this knowledge into your daily plans. If you're not a morning person then ease yourself in with bite-sized tasks that are easy to get through and don't require intense concentration, saving your meatier tasks for later in the day. If you find yourself brimming with new ideas and feeling revived by your lunch break, then plan in any creative activities for when you get back to your desk. Struggle to keep your eyes open over dinner with your mates on a week night? Then pencil in your catch-ups for the weekend instead. Maybe Mondays are the day you feel like your energy peaks? Or perhaps it's Wednesday when you feel at your sharpest? Factor these peaks and troughs in, too. This dialogue between yourself, your attention and your energy levels will help you create plans for your day, week or month ahead with the highest chance of successfully executing them.

STEP #2: BE REALISTIC

Your plan for the working day should make you feel peaceful. I know it sounds too good to be true, and there will be times when it doesn't exactly *scream* serenity, but if you can reach a place where the majority of your daily plans don't come with a side order of stress and increased blood pressure, then we're all good. Think of your plan like your mate who dishes out kind, thoughtful and gentle advice, not the one who shouts 'WHY THE HELL WOULD YOU WANT TO DO THAT?' at you. Although the latter type of friend does come in really handy when you're about to make a bloody awful decision, being around the former feels like a lovely, warm hug, right? So, for the most part, having a plan in your hand should make you feel organised and give you purpose, like a supportive arm round your shoulder, not a palm-crunching handshake. Let's not forget the pillars of self-care, eh? Be nice to yourself! The main way to safeguard this is to make sure that whatever tasks you set yourself are realistic within the timeframe you set. It sounds so simple but we are all generally over-optimistic with how quickly we think we can get a task completed. It's a skill that can be learnt only though trial and error, and it might never be truly perfected. But once you get close, I can pretty much guarantee that you'll be setting yourself plans that are low on stress, sympathetic to your daily energy levels and that you'll actually find yourself getting through.

If you're struggling to get a grip on how long tasks are taking you to complete, then run yourself through this extra bit of homework before you get to creating your schedule:

1   In an Excel, Numbers or Google Sheet document, break your working day down into hourly slots, vertically in the first column. Repeat this for every working day you have in a week, so you create yourself a timesheet.

2   For a one-week period, fill in how long it takes you to complete tasks. If sorting through your inbox takes an hour, but writing up and actioning meeting notes takes three – add these in.

3   At the end of the week, take a flick back through the timesheet and look at how long each task took. Surprised by the results? Make a note of tasks that took longer or shorter than you expected, and use this information when it comes to setting down your concentrated plan for the following week ahead.

STEP #3: ZOOM OUT AND ZOOM IN

We've covered the basics to consider before you deep-dive into planning, but now it's time to stop faffing and begin working on how to structure your working day in a way that's optimal for you. Here's what we're looking to achieve.

A good plan for a working day will:

- Make you feel cool, calm and collected, not panicked.

- Set tasks for you to complete within a realistic timeframe.

- Take into account how your energy levels fluctuate.

In terms of setting out your working day, begin with the bigger blocks and work your way down to the smaller ones, just like you did with setting your goals. Duplo down to the tiny bits of Lego that elicit a pain like no other if you ever stand on them. Here's what we're going to do:

- Monthly, we're going to consult our calendars for any major projects, events or long-term deadlines.

- Weekly, we'll keep track of monthly to-do tasks (and set them to recurring in our calendars if we haven't already).

- Once a week, we'll assess our diaries for the next seven days and plan our daily tasks from there, remembering to be realistic with our time and lean in to our personal energy levels where possible.

EVERY WEEK – CHECK RECURRING TASKS

Once you've absorbed your yearly view, do one click to zoom in on the upcoming month. My guess is that there are probably work-related tasks that are non-negotiable and have to be completed monthly. For me that's things relating to accounting and finance, certain updates that I make on my blog on a monthly basis, compiling my monthly newsletter and any additional projects that need addressing. Although these are more traditional to-do list items, seeing as they are recurring I plan them into my digital calendar and set them up to be automatically added in monthly. This way the diary alerts act as a reminder so I don't forget them, and as I plan out my weeks I reference my calendar, so I know when to add them in as an actual to-do list task, ready to be completed.

ONCE A WEEK – ZOOM IN TO THE NEXT SEVEN DAYS

Here's where the proper to-do list takes shape. So far all the planning moves we've made have been either in your digital or paper calendar. We've added in any major deadlines that are due over the course of the next year and we've set any must-do monthly tasks to automatically recur. Working down to the next smallest chunk, take a snapshot of your upcoming week. What meetings have you got on? Any deadlines looming? Lunches? Dinners? Training events? I'm old-school when it comes to my plan, and opt for jotting down to-do lists in my notepad, but if you prefer to do it digitally I recommend Evernote and Todoist, and monday.com is great for any planning that you might want to share with others in your team.

Reaching the daily planning stage is a universal technique. It just makes sense for us all to use, and having this macro zooming in to the micro approach means that nothing work-wise gets through the net – and knowing what we've got coming up should help with the ol' stress levels. When it comes to breaking it down into your weekly and daily plans, it's going to be different for everyone – and just like your calendar choice in the first chapter, it might take a few gos to find *The One*.

STEP #4: SET UP YOUR PLANNING FRAMEWORK

My tasks tend to be snappy and more short-term focused, and so a paper list in a Bullet Journal format works really well for me (don't worry, we'll get to those in a second). But if you tend to have longer projects, then a system like Trello – where you can keep tabs on multiple to-do lists over any period of time – might be a better option. I have a friend who just plans for the day ahead on a super-snappy basis. She keeps a pad of paper on a clipboard, and any tasks that she doesn't complete she carries over to the next day, just adding points down as they arise. The Notes app on your phone is a good planning tool, too. Especially if you're on the go, don't find yourself at a desk often and aren't too into the idea of organising in a pen and paper kinda way. Of course you could just use the 'three-*ish* tasks a day' option like I do, but I have a friend who likes to plan her day to the hour. The evening before, she sits down and types up her agenda for the day ahead from action points that she's added in her calendar, and gives herself an hourly to-do list for the next 24 hours. All of these are methods that work for those individuals; there's no wrong or right way to set out your plan. Here are some options to try:

PAPER	APPS	OTHER METHODS
Plan a **week to a page**, setting yourself a handful of condensed tasks to complete a day.	**Asana** – For use as either an individual or a team, here you can keep track of workflow, timelines and to-do list points.	It's not exactly the sexiest app, but **Notes** or whatever version you have, is a quick and easy way to make a to-do list in seconds.
Plan a **day to a page**, giving yourself a breakdown of your to-do list action points.	**Todoist** – A way of organising jumbled action plans into something that's manageable and more plan-like. Perfect for planning big projects.	**monday.com** is a planning place for teams. You can schedule and assign tasks, update progress and add in timelines for team members.
Use a page as a **daily to-do list**, ticking items off and adding items still left to complete the following day on the next page.	**Evernote** – So simple, it's basically like a Bullet Journal (a to-do list and calendar in one) but in digital form. A one-stop organisational shop.	**Trello** – A great tool to use for those who are managing multiple projects at any time. It's to-do list central and easy to keep track of.

Whichever one sings to you is the one to try. Maybe you'll find it revolutionises the way you plan. You feel great! You're getting stuff done! You discover a new-found appreciation for tick boxes! Maybe you don't. If that's the case and it really isn't working for you, then tweak, edit or just push it to the side – and try something new.

How I plan my working day

I've honed my technique over years, and now I tend to do my scheduling either on a Friday evening (if I'm feeling *real* organised), sometime over the weekend if the planning bug bites, or on a Monday morning.

I first consult my iCal calendar, then set out my weekly schedule in a notepad which is *kind of* a Bullet Journal. I write the days of the week down on one page and then I write each to-do list item, prefaced with a dot that can be crossed through when it's completed, under the relevant day. As I said, I find that less specific, more general points work better for me instead of a detailed list, as it tricks my mind into feeling like the workload for the day is more manageable, so I only ever write up to four, possibly five maximum, action points. I try to take into account how I think I will feel motivation-wise throughout the week, and plan tasks that require higher levels of focus in the mornings and more creative things in the afternoons. If I have a day of meetings and I know my energy will be sucked into that, I will fill the rest of the day up with things that don't require me to move from my desk. If I have a day in London where I know I'll be away from my laptop for the majority of the working day, I'll set myself things that can be done in the morning before I leave, or tasks that I can complete on my phone on the go. It's all about moulding your tasks and adapting their order around the chunks of time that you have available. Here's what a weekly to-do list looks like for me:

- Schedule social media posts for the week ahead

- Edit workspace chapter for *An Edited Life*

- Think up and prep ideas for tomorrow's blog photography shoot

- Shoot blog photography pictures

- Sort out expenses

- Edit planning chapter for *An Edited Life*

- Write 1,000 words of next *An Edited Life* chapter

- Make sure inbox is clear by E.O.D.

- Add blog photography pictures into posts and scheduled social media posts

- Write 'BTS of the Podcast' blog post

- Write 'Summer Dressing' blog post

- Write 'Reading Recommendations' blog post

- Make notes for next 'At Home With...' podcast guest

- Vlog the day for upcoming YouTube video

- Edit and schedule the video

- Finish off productivity chapter for *An Edited Life*

As long as you are arranging your time in a way that makes you feel in control and keeps your stress levels manageable, then you're acing this whole planning thing. *It's all smooth sailing from here baby!* Well, *kinda*. The factors that can derail us are going to be different triggers for us all, but here's how to troubleshoot the two most frequent set-backs that can really screw up our time-management skills – deadlines and an inbox from hell.

How to stick to deadlines

All tasks that we set ourselves to complete as part of the planning process are going to have some kind of deadline. Perhaps it's self-imposed – without a feeling of urgency we'd never get round to it – or the due date is set by an external factor. Either way there's something about the word *deadline* that instils a fear in us, second only to that time your friends made you sit through the whole of *The Shining* when you were only 11 (and you're still haunted by it. *I feel you*). We all have deadlines that are so regular that we don't even think about them. I post on my blog three times a week, and so by 9am on a Monday, Wednesday and Friday I need to make sure that there's a post ready to go. It's a routine I've had in place for so many years that, although the workload can pile up from time to time, I don't tend to stress about the actual deadline because it's so frequent. However, I get the tight feeling at the back of my throat creep in with bigger projects, especially ones that I haven't done before. Say, like, writing a book for example… You might find it the same. With tasks that you complete regularly, you can switch into automatic mode, but when new projects crop up, all of a sudden the deadline becomes an important factor that looms and can often manifest in increased feelings of '*Maybe it's time to give meditation a go again?*' levels of anxiousness.

SO YOU HAVE A DEADLINE?

FIRST Deadlines need to be realistic. If you're already wondering just how few hours of sleep it's possible to live off until the deadline drops, then it's probably time to have a rethink. Sure, short turnarounds always crop up; it might be part of the job and perhaps it's not always possible to push back on timings. In those cases I'd suggest re-jigging your plans for the week, and prioritising tasks and putting those with the least importance completely off your plate so you have less to focus on overall. Don't be afraid to speak up and manage expectations from beginning, plus provide feedback once it's completed to avoid the same tight schedule being proposed again.

SECOND Once the date is pinned down, add the important timestamps to your diary. This is a good point to take stock, so step back to look at the overall outcome, break it down into chunks and to-do list points that need to be completed. Work out how to factor that into your weekly planning in the correct timeframe to get it finished by the deadline. Write these specific tasks down as part of a separate sub-list, either a separate page in your Bullet Journal or notepad, or their very own tab in whatever software you use, so you can refer back to this master list each time you set yourself a weekly plan. To effectively time-manage the project I like to add in monthly or weekly check-in reminders to my calendar. For any tasks that span across a month I like to add in weekly milestones to hit so I can make sure that I'm not getting behind, and if we're talking a task taking months or possibly a year, then I'd suggest adding a reminder in your calendar monthly with a note of tasks that you expect to be completed by that time.

THIRD Begin right away if you can. The thing with long-term deadlines is that our brain does a really good job of forgetting about them until they're, like, *next week* – forcing us into panic mode. So give yourself a head start. Why not? Beginning a task is the hardest bit, so by getting that out of the way as quickly as possible you're instantly decreasing the chance of procrastination taking hold.

When it comes to deadlines and completing tasks within the allotted time without having to pull all-nighters or leaving yourself an immense amount of work to complete in an immensely short period of time, it's all about visibility. The more reminders there are about something, the less you'll be able to bat it away. The combination of calendar alerts, separate to-do lists and giving yourself a head start, will all help to ease any stress you feel about impending deadlines. Keeping them at the forefront of your mind, being organised and methodical about the steps needed to complete them, and getting yourself over the hurdle of actually starting, will mean that missed deadlines aren't even on the cards. Don't bury them away – instead consistently chip away at them. Speaking of buried, are you currently trying to dig your way out of email inbox hell? I have some pointers up my sleeve.

How to deal with emails

Oh, emails. They're both the best modern addition to the workplace and the worst. They connect us to others and allow us to communicate clearly, but then they also connect us to others who are constantly trying to coerce us into buying penis enlargement pills. You see? They're both brilliant and exceptionally grim at the same time. Emails are the one thing that we're all united on. We all have a handful of addresses (including the 'lil_miss_minx_69' one that you set up when you were 15) and we all have an inbox. Even my 78-year-old grandad has one! But the reason why it needs a whole dedicated section of its own in *An Edited Life* is that there's a high chance that the vicious circle of replying and receiving is a major drain on your time and planning resources. Once you factor in livechat, WhatsApp and a slew of conference calls, it's a miracle that we ever get anything done at work at all.

We might all have an inbox, but when it comes to dealing with them there are three camps. There are the people who start to breathe heavily when their inboxes reach double digits and can't sleep until it's back down to zero. That's me. What a surprise. There are those who probably sit around the mark of having about 20–30 emails to reply to at any time, and although your process could do with a little editing, it's nothing you can't handle. Then there are those who have 12,387 unread emails and don't even know where to start. That final one goes out to my mate Flora who actually does have that number of unread emails, only trumped by my friend Katie who once had 20,000+. I've seen it with my own eyes and yes, I did almost faint.

Once you get to that point there's nothing else you can do aside from use the search function to fish out any important emails you need to reference, file them away and then hit the 'delete all' button for the rest. When you've done that, come back and join the group, because no matter what the state of your inbox is, I've got some methods you can deploy that should help to ease the load a little.

Before you implement the one that tickles your fancy, let's do a bit of inbox hygiene. Tick off the following. Does your inbox contain:

- Folders that make emails easy to track down when you need them and that groups ones with a similar topic in the same place?

- Flags or tags on any emails that still require action – again, giving them priority and making them easy to view in one window?

- A signature that contains your name, title and any relevant links? SO PROFESH.

- An organised inbox that only contains emails from the past 24 hours?

- Saved templates for any emails where you regularly find yourself submitting the same response (seriously, these are life-changing!)?

- An out-of-office response that's clear, concise and easy to turn on and off?

If the answer is no to any of these questions then you know what to do. This self-check spring clean will ensure you're organised from the get-go, and not just attempting to polish a turd. Although some of these practices might take a bit of time and be a little fiddly to set up, they all allow for more automation and time-saving at your end in the long run, which should mean that there's less time in your schedule spent untangling the mess in your inbox, and more time spent ticking through your to-do list.

Once you've blown away the cobwebs from the depths of your inbox and installed some order into your folders, it's time to work on a method that makes the process of sending and receiving emails dreamy. Depending on your role, frequency of emails, and the priority they have in the day-to-day running of your job, how you deal with your inbox is going to be slightly different, but the following three methods are fully ready to be tweaked and tuned as required.

The common issue that we can all agree on is that we're a slave to our inboxes. The constant pinging sound or flashing red alert that something has arrived and is desperate to be read that interrupts our flow and robs us of any shred of focus we had. Unless we're waiting for a life-altering email to fly into our inboxes, the chances are that whatever is waiting there for a reply can wait another hour until you've finished up whatever you're working on, *right?* So these three techniques should help you to manage your time more effectively and therefore do the same for your inbox too…

IF YOU CAN'T EVER FINISH A TASK BECAUSE YOU GET DISTRACTED BY EVERY EMAIL THAT COMES IN: **SET TO PUSH**
I'd recommend doing this step whatever route you decide to take with your inbox, but by setting your emails to fetch whenever you open the app, instead of retrieving messages all day long, will help to compartmentalise the task. I set my mobile to battery-saving mode during the week and that means that I need to refresh my inbox manually whenever I open the app in order to see what's new in there. Then on my desktop I keep the app closed and only open it when I actually have time to deal with whatever I might find. Just the fact that you don't have a red number on your homepage steadily increasing by the hour, and notifications popping up at the side of the screen when you're in the flow of another task, make emails seem a whole lot easier to deal with. It's simple, but effective.

IF EMAILS FLOOD IN AND YOU CAN'T FOCUS ON ONE MESSAGE: **THE 'THREE TIMES A DAY' RULE**
Once you've set your inbox to only retrieve messages when you tell it to, you can go one step further and set yourself a timetable of when in your day it's best to do that. If you're working well on your own schedule, then plough on, but if you feel like you're still checking it multiple times a day and find yourself looking at a heap of unanswered emails, then it's time to edit in an extra level of organisation. In this case I'd recommend the *'three times a day'* rule. You check your inbox once in the morning and reply to anything that has come in the previous evening or overnight, then once around lunchtime to do a tidy-up of any urgent morning messages, then do one final check just before you clock off for the day to reply to whatever is left. This is how I personally like to approach my inbox. By checking it three times a day I'm able to keep on top of it, and I don't feel like it ever gets too overwhelming. Short and sharp bursts work better for me, plus I'm able

to catch anything in the net that's urgent in a timely fashion. It's about finding those slots of time for you, where you feel like tackling your inbox won't soak up any super-focused juice that could be better used on other tasks. You want to make your check-ins as short and sweet as possible and at times that don't eat into times when you're getting into really meaty to-do list items.

IF REPLYING TO YOUR EMAILS TAKES ALL DAY AND YOU CAN'T GET ANYTHING ELSE DONE: **A DESIGNATED REPLY TIME**

More and more I receive automatically generated responses to emails I send, from recipients who have a designated reply time for their emails. Some only answer emails on a Monday, Wednesday and Friday. Or just twice a week? Or even at 9am every morning? Whatever their designated reply time rules are, they put it in their email signatures and have an automatic reply – a bit like an out-of-office – that lets people in on this and so they know when to expect a reply. Often there will also be a number to call if you need to find something out more urgently. I think this is a win-win for everyone. Those who set these sorts of rules for themselves do so in order to ease the stress of dealing with their inboxes and to free up more time for other endeavours; and those on the receiving end are kept in the loop and so won't get angsty when a reply takes longer than expected. If you feel like this is something that could work for you and your role, just remember to set up your inbox so an automatic message that details your email strategy goes out to all who email you. A simple: '*Just a quick note, to keep productivity at a maximum I only check emails on a Monday, Wednesday and Friday, so please bear with me. Your business is very important to me and I will get back to you as soon as I can*' is a good template to use.

Use whatever method you feel works best for you, but editing an email routine into your working day will help you to block out your time more effectively, and to stick to your plans with increased focus on the tasks that you actually need to get done. Spending hours feeling lost in a sea of emails doesn't need to be something that happens daily, or ever again, and surely that's the best perk of an edited life yet?

So you have your planning blueprint down and you've got the tips to safeguard for possible bumps in the road, but is there a way that perfectly ties up everything we've covered about time management and scheduling? Well, it's funny that you should ask…

What the hell are Bullet Journals?

They're trendy old things, these Bullet Journals. If you're already a seasoned pro at this whole organisation malarkey then the chances are that you've already heard of them and have probably Bullet Journalled your way through multiple notebooks already. However, if you're new to the game, let me explain.

At its core a Bullet Journal is a to-do list, planner and diary all in one, that primarily uses bullet-point lists throughout to organise – hence the name. If you're someone who likes the idea of a planner, finds stationery shops oddly arousing and has a sea of to-do lists floating around on post-it notes, then this might be a solution for you. All you need is an empty notebook and a pen, and you're good to go.

There are whole books dedicated to the method created by Ryder Carroll, but I've read them for you and already prepped the crib notes, so I'll try and make it snappy. If you do fancy giving them a read for yourself, then head to the **Resources** section for my recommendations. In terms of layout, your long-term planning is formatted at the beginning of your Bullet Journal, followed by shorter-term planning and daily to-do lists. You start big and then you get down to the granular detail – just like I've suggested. Here's the five-step plan to get you started:

HOW TO CREATE A BULLET JOURNAL

1   Number every single page in your notebook like you would a book. Easy peasy.

2   Create a contents page at the front of the book, by writing the page numbers vertically down the margin. As you fill out your Bullet Journal, you begin each new page with a title that's easily recognisable, you then add this to the relevant page number in your contents page, and voilà – all your notes, lists and scribbles should be easy to find.

3   Your 'Future Log' is next and is where you'll store information regarding long-term projects. Take the next four pages and split each page into three. You'll end up with 12 sections that you can head up with the months of the year. Leave it empty for now. Add it to your contents page.

4   The next double-page is your first 'Monthly Log', which shows you everything that you have on over the coming four weeks. On the left-hand page write the month as the heading and put the dates in the margins. In the original method it's not really used for much aside from being a visual calendar, but I find that it's handy to use for any important dates, birthdays and events. On the right-hand page write any major tasks you need to get done that month and their completion date. Make a note of the page numbers and remember to add them into your contents page, for example: pp12–13 'Monthly Log – *Insert month here*'.

5   Turn the page and begin your first 'Daily Log', which is a simply list of tasks to get done in the next 24 hours. Header up the page with the date and begin writing your to-do list for the day ahead. Remember to keep scanning back to the 'Monthly Log' to make sure you're ticking everything off as the month progresses. Continue doing this daily, until you get to the end of the month. Here you'll

begin a new 'Monthly Log' – remember to consult the old one and transfer unfinished tasks to either the 'Future Log' or your new month list, then continue on with your 'Daily Logs' after it.

6 You can leave it there, or you can add in your own logs and lists tailored to your individual needs. The major pull of the Bullet Journal is that it's a fully customisable organisation method. A log for meal planning? Capsule wardrobe shopping lists? A workout log? A list of TV programmes that you'd like to watch? Restaurants you want to visit? A Bullet Journal can be the home for any nugget of information or list that you fancy, and the more you tailor it, the more helpful it can be in your life-editing process.

Up to this point it just sounds like a pretty standard, well-organised notebook, but where the method really gets serious is with the key. Of course you can create your own, but I'll talk you through the official Bullet Journal version in case you want to stick to the rules. A to-do list item in any of your three logs is symbolised with a bullet point that you then cross through when you mark it as complete. The 'more than' symbol (>) can be drawn over a bullet if the task still needs to be completed but is due months from now and you've yet to set a to-do date for it. Draw this symbol over the bullet and write the task into the relevant month in the 'Future Log' so you don't forget it. See? That's where it comes in. The 'less than' symbol (<) is again drawn over if you've yet to complete the task but you have moved it to another day and into another 'Daily Log'. Dashes can be used for notes and a big open circle (o) for events like birthdays or social occasions.

●	to-do list item
×	completed to-do list item
>	not completed, unscheduled
<	not completed, but scheduled
–	notes
o	events

BULLET DOS:

- The contents page might seem like a drag to set up, but it has actually helped me find many missing notes over the years. Just make sure you make it a habit to keep it up to date.

- Keep a ruler handy. It sounds odd, but I actually use mine most days to split a page into two or to underline a heading. Yes, I know I could freehand, but HELLO – MONICA HERE!

- Get creative. If doing the odd doodle here and there or writing in different colour pens for different lists is tipping your productiveness/procrastination scales in the right direction, then be my guest. If you fancy doing the whole thing in blue pen, like me, then welcome to the club.

BULLET DON'TS:

- If your tasks are more short-term orientated, ditch the 'Future Log'. It became an empty space for me as I just don't plan that far ahead editorially.

- Don't feel like you have to stick to the rules. I've found that creating my own key has worked best for me, and although I love the bullets, crosses and dashes, I don't bother with the more than/less than symbols as I don't operate a 'Future Log'.

- Try not to feel too precious about being neat. You obviously want to be able to read your lists easily, but you're not creating the world's next Picasso here.

It's a lot to take in, right? It's a Marmite idea, and while it works brilliantly for some people, it's a complete failure for others and interest will wane after approximately three days. Personally, I use a mix of both iCal and Bullet Journal to schedule both my life and work. I tend to keep all date-specific items on my digital calendar and so they are easy to move around and see at a glance, and then plan most of my work-related projects and content in my Bullet Journal, as I'm a sucker for an old-school tick – *sorry, cross* – once a task is complete. After years of fumbling around with different methods, half-completed diaries and missed birthdays, I've found it's what works best for me and keeps me at my most efficient, non-birthday-missing self.

I really do believe that although we need to be flexible with a plan, and although it doesn't always work out quite how we imagined, buoying yourself up with one helps with that sort of 'heavy' feeling that we get from time to time when bogged down by our responsibilities. Of course, the alleviation of that is the result of combining most, if not all, of the chapters in this book – but planning really helps to form the start of that reaction.

The Edit

Seeing as planning is a key belief of an edited life, and such a fundamental piece of the puzzle that I honestly would feel pretty lost without, this chapter was always going to be a hefty one.

By implementing the techniques covered in this chapter you'll see how a well-thought-out and realistic plan allows you to dump must-dos out of our brains and onto paper or into apps, to create more space for us to focus on completing tasks. The section that covers our energy levels is a really good one to remind yourself of frequently, especially if getting your work done feels like you're trying to fit a circle into a square. It's such a simple premise but it's one that we don't reference often enough. It happens to us all, and if we just took notice of it and listened a little more, we'd be much more likely to stick with what we've set out. Of course, now you're also an inbox pro with your own email bossing routine. I'm not a stickler for the rules (if you are, don't ever watch my measuring when I bake - it's likely that my laissez-faire attitude with ingredient measuring could be the demise of my marriage), but being stern with myself when it comes to dealing with my inbox has rocked my world. Being as regimented as you can with it will enable you to plough through your plans without noise and pinging as your own personal backing track.

Now you've got the planning side of your work life down, it's time to turn your attention to the processes that are worth putting in place to actually see them through. It's all well and good talking the talk - *you've got the colour-coded schedule and all!* - but from time to time we all find ourselves struggling to walk the walk, and lacking the motivation we need to see something through. Luckily, I have more than a few tricks up my sleeve to put procrastination to bed. Let's turn that on its head and learn how to have the other 'P' word - *productiveness* - triumph.

You'll be ticking tasks off in no time...

How to get tasks done

You've carved a well-thought-out schedule, so now it's time to put that plan into practice in a way that embraces maximum levels of productivity and keeps procrastination to a minimum.

You've created goals, turned them into a plan, built a schedule for yourself and identified the best order for your to-do list, and now you have to start actually ticking it off. The spreadsheets, the word documents, the editing, the telephone calls, the meetings, the research, the reading, the revision. Planning is the easy bit, now it's time to get to the grind. I will admit that the following chapter is as much for my benefit as it is for yours. Planning is my strong point – my homework diary was FLAWLESS – but procrastination has always been a strength of mine too, which means that my '*Anna is easily distracted*' school reports are just as applicable now as they were 20 years ago. Before settling down to write this chapter I found myself sunken into a YouTube hole watching highlights from an episode of *Love Island* that was aired three years ago, which then led me to a half-hour-long bikini buying scroll session and then booking into an extra session of Pilates this week. HELP. I only picked up my laptop when the battery on my phone flicked to zero and I finally resigned myself to the universe telling me that it was time to get back into work mode (and because I couldn't be bothered to cross the room to plug my phone back in – laziness and procrastination? What a winning combo!).

If procrastination isn't a problem for you and you are efficiency personified, like my mate Mel who I am sure is the most beautiful, work-loving, kind and funny robot that I have ever met, then two for you Glen Coco! However, if you find yourself using your belly as a laptop rest and doing your fourth 'How well do you know **insert the name of a popular TV programme here*?*' quiz of the day, then this chapter is packed with advice from how I have taught myself to take my time-wasting activities down a level or two so I actually get stuff done. *Sometimes*. I've been there, done that, watched six seasons of *RuPaul's Drag Race* in two weeks so you don't have to. *You'd. Better. Work.*

LACK OF MOTIVATION + DISTRACTIONS =
PROCRASTINATION

HIGH LEVELS OF MOTIVATION + MINIMAL DISTRACTIONS =
PRODUCTIVITY

Procrastination can rear its ugly head when motivation is scarce, but that's not the only root of the problem. In the modern world, where distractions crop up as often as a brand-new, long and extremely black chin hair, we're often led down the work-shy path which leads to lost minutes, hours and whole stretches of afternoons. We're no longer just wasting time worrying about whether our mum has cleared away our Tamagotchi's poop while we've been at school; instead, our ability to focus is tested by a gazillion factors – *Did we turn the straighteners off? Why does a one-bed flat cost the price of a unicorn? Has a new 'Ryan Gosling Best Bits' video been uploaded to YouTube? When are our parents going to stop trying to add us on Facebook?* So when you throw distractions into the equation with lacking motivation levels, procrastination goes from being a possibility to being inevitable. The 'Ryan Gosling Best Bits' black hole opens right up and the chances of a return before the end of the day are slim pickings.

Instead we have to turn the equation on its head. When we flip it and combine motivation levels that are bubbling over the top with minimal distractions, then we find our happy place when it comes to work flow. Along with identifying our motivation kick-starters, it's worth learning some methods to stall procrastination in its tracks and turn it into the more preferable 'p word' – and that's what this chapter will provide for you. It's all about fewer cute-dog videos and more boxes being ticked, which certainly isn't as adorable, but boy does it feel good to get shit done…

Lacking motivation? Let's find it...

Motivation can sometimes be a fleeting thing. Like a cat that only makes an appearance when there's food involved, and once it has eaten disappears back under the bed and into a corner that's humanly impossible to reach. Or that moment after a bikini wax where you feel so free and fast, like you'd be able to set a world record in a sprint, only to have a six-o'clock-shadow two days later (*did I tell you that my father is Wolverine?*). It's an elusive thing; sometimes we're feeling it and sometimes we're not. So in our search for motivation, firstly let's try to turn it into something that we can grab onto with both hands, so it isn't as likely to slip through our fingers and out of our grips so easily. Learning to identify your own personal motivators – and which situations to apply them to – is your insurance policy to fall back on in moments when your drive to do stuff is wavering/completely non-existent.

It's the equivalent of retracing your footsteps. When you've lost your keys you revisit everything you've done in the run-up to discovering their misplacement. You search through items you've used, rooms you've been in, decide that they're gone forever, spend £20 on cutting a new pair, then promptly find them on your return from the locksmith in that back pocket of your bag that you never use. Let's just say that I haven't used that pocket since – but I've learnt my lesson! By doing the same process and analysing our motivation levels when they're both sky-high and down in the dumps, we should be able to notice a pattern and be able to decipher the key factors that play a part in both situations.

Next time you're feeling like you're riding the wave of motivation like a pro surfer and not someone who didn't even stand up last time they went paddle boarding (THAT'S ME!), take a couple of minutes to write down in your notepad or on your phone the five reasons why you feel you're in this state, taking into account both internal and external factors.

- Is it the task that you're doing?

- Have you nourished your body well?

- Is it the fact that you had a good night's sleep last night?

- Or that you've got your inbox down to zero?

- Or that you caught up with friends last night and are just in a good mood?

- The good weather?

- Is the office murmur at just the right background volume?

- Is it the lack of any noise at all?

Repeat the exact same exercise but when your procrastination levels are off the chart. I'm talking like three hours deep into a Shane Dawson series *extreme*.

- Are you confused about the task you've been set?

- Have you nourished your body at all today?

- Did you struggle to sleep last night?

- Is your inbox STRESSING. YOU. OUT?

- What have your social interactions been like over the past couple of days?

- Is the weather shit?

- Is the office murmur too loud?

- Is it too weird and silent for you to get your head down?

By deciphering your own individual triggers for both a highly motivated and a procrastination-heavy state, you have yourself a personalised ingredient card for both recipes. You'll have five things to try in order to revisit your 'in the flow' moment, and then five things to avoid when you're just not feeling it.

Of course, some of these might be out of your control – good weather unfortunately isn't something that we have much of a handle on – but the chances are that there will be some that are actionable, so mark or highlight these ones. Next time you're low on the motivation spectrum, look to one of these factors and dial it up. Even if it's just turning your knob from 0 to 25%, it's better than nothing, eh?

These scenarios are going to be different for everyone. While I work best in complete and utter silence (which makes it great when the neighbour is having building work done), my husband prefers to listen to loud rock music in his ears *shudders*. So maybe you thrive off stressful last-minute deadlines, or maybe even just the idea of that gives you a bout of IBS? We're all special snowflakes so my sweet spots may not be the same as yours, but in the interest of giving food for thought, here are some places that I go to find motivation when my hunger for work is taking a hit…

What I do when I'm...

LACKING MOTIVATION TO CREATE

When my creative juices are low I become a sponge for content that inspires me. I carve out 30 minutes of my schedule just to consume: to snoop around online, read a book, flick through a magazine, visit a blog, watch a video or listen to a podcast and fully engage with it without multi-tasking. By giving myself a short window of time it keeps me off the procrastination path, and focused and on-task, seeking out inspiration and squeezing out the rest. There's something about dipping my toe in the content ocean that perks me right up.

Sometimes it might trigger an idea that I'd already had but completely forgotten, or it will make me think of something new to create that I haven't done before. Not only do I find it enjoyable and actually pretty relaxing, nine times out of ten a cracking idea comes from it.

- Move your work into a new space by switching rooms or working from a public place.

- Commit to creating something every day, like writing a poem for 100 days on the trot, or posting a daily video. Sometimes forcing ourselves to repeatedly do something creates something insanely amazing and builds our confidence, which in turn ups our creativity.

LACKING MOTIVATION BECAUSE I FEEL STRESSED

Sometimes I feel like my motivation is being cut off because I feel stressed. This heart-pounding, anxiety-ridden state isn't conducive to productivity and it's something that can affect all of us from time to time. No one is immune to stress, but there are ways to manage it and lessen the load, so that's exactly what I do whenever it stands in the way of my workload. The chances are that I'm feeling stressed because I've been too optimistic with my planning, so I work priority into the mix. I put high-priority items at the top of the list, with other things that aren't so time sensitive being put to the side temporarily until I'm feeling back in peak performance mode. This ironing out of my plans is a sure-fire way to up my productivity levels, and allows space for motivation to worm its way back into my working day.

- Get out of the house. Go for a walk to clear your head; not only will it play into the 'move more' pillar of self-care, if you take your mates along with you or go for a wander with colleagues, the interaction will bolster you up too.

- Sometimes stress can actually work as a motivator – you want the feeling to decrease and the only way to do that is to complete those tasks that are making you feel that way. Turn the negative into a positive and ride it out.

LACKING MOTIVATION ON A PARTICULAR DEADLINE OR TASK

I'll put my hands up and say that long-term tasks aren't my strength in the workplace. Short and snappy blog posts? LOVELY JUBBLY. But projects that span the course of a couple of months, even years? Say, like writing a book? LOLZ. Keeping up motivation over a long stretch of time is basically an endurance sport and so we should treat it like one. Just like our energy levels naturally ebb and flow, our motivation for a particular task will do exactly the same. So some days you might write a chapter and other days it's a struggle to write 100 words. I find that the best way to sustain some kind of motivational thrill in these instances is to set myself a daily goal to reach. You might like to keep it the same goal to hit every day, or maybe you find it's more of a motivator for you if it's slightly different every day. Make sure that it's realistic and workable around your other commitments so that it won't loom over you. Write it up in your notepad, or print it out and stick it above your desk – just make sure that it's easily viewable and will act as a daily reminder. Ticking off your daily goal should help to buoy up your motivation levels, and you'll get there slowly but surely.

ALTERNATIVE IDEAS:

- Talk it out with a friend. They might have some fresh ideas for your project or be able to share some tips on how they tackled their last deadline that they thought they'd never hit. A problem shared is a problem halved, and all that.

- Some of us need the deadline to be looming in order to get us moving, and that's fine. Just make sure that your diary is set up to accommodate that, and do any prep and research well in advance so you're ready to get to it when motivation hits.

LACKING MOTIVATION TO DO ANYTHING

I know this sounds dramatic, but do you ever have moments when you lack the drive to do anything? YUP. I flick through my phone ∟ BORING. I look through my cupboards for something to eat and there's nothing there. I pick up my laptop, delete some junk emails and then immediately close it again because I've remembered that there's ice cream in the freezer. Nope, turns out my husband ate it secretly last night when I was out. Maybe I'll read? Oh wait, I've just read the first line of the first page 47 times and I still couldn't tell you what it said. You've been there too? I feel you. It's a prime example of an utter lack of ability to focus, and in those moments where I just 'can't/really don't want to do' anything, I tap out. I go for a walk, I book in for a workout session ASAP; the act of removing myself from my place of work – even just for 15 minutes – acts as a hard reset on *everything*. I understand that this is an easier scenario for those who work at home or have flexible working hours, but even if you can just step away from your desk to pour yourself a drink and take the long way back to your seat, it helps. Fresh air works a particular kind of magic, but just a mini break to get your legs moving and the cogs on your wheel of motivation turning again, does wonders.

ALTERNATIVE IDEAS:

- Sometimes it's just an off day, so strive for tomorrow to be a better one. Set yourself a plan, factor in some movement, make sure you're all set up for food and SMASH IT.

- Put 10 minutes on the clock and do something work related. Anything. 10 minutes is so short that it's practically impossible not to be able to fill that length of time productively.

LACKING MOTIVATION TO LOOK AFTER MYSELF

I am a junk food addict. If it was medically advised to eat a burger and chips twice a day, topped off with a slice of pizza and half a tub of ice cream, I could do it. *Easy*. I occasionally get the taste for something green which I would quite like to bottle up and drip-feed myself daily, but it passes fast, and once a couple of leaves have made it in, my hunger for nutritional value fades. So looking after myself when it comes to food and fitness is something that I have to work on and gee up my motivation for. It's a vicious circle when my impetus is running low, as I eat pants, feel pants and therefore nourish myself with more biscuits. So in order to break the cycle I give myself the goal of ticking all the right boxes for just one day. I make sure I've got food in to cook myself, I meal-plan, book in a Pilates session and ensure I've got plenty of homemade snacks around to nibble on. *Surprise surprise*, the one day of eating varied, home-cooked meals with fruit and veg (!!!) makes me feel fab and energised and puts a spring back in my step, pushing me on to repeat the same tomorrow – the spell finally broken.

- A brand-spanking-new cookbook is a game-changer whenever I'm feeling tired in the kitchen. New recipes! New ideas! You'll want to make them all.

- Cooking can be a great stress reliever, so invite your friends over for a hearty and tasty meal that isn't just pizza cooked up in the oven. They'll be grateful for a lovely dinner and you can all share your favourite healthy hacks and ideas.

We'll all have different action points that remedy our lack of motivation in various scenarios, but hopefully these have provided the basics that you can clip onto your tool belt to put in use whenever you need to repair it. All you need is to taste how good it feels when it begins sparking again, then before you know it the floodgates are flung open. The weight has been lifted off your shoulders and you're working through your plans like there's no tomorrow. There's steam coming off your laptop keyboard. GO YOU! So your motivation mojo is back! Now, if we can work out how to dim our appetites for procrastination, then we're *really* onto something.

How to stall procrastination

Once we've worked out where to search when our motivation levels are dipping, it's time to sort out the other half of the equation and learn how to suppress our appetites for distractions and the procrastination that accompanies them.

I've mentioned already that it's my edited life sore spot, and working from home doesn't exactly help my mid-afternoon urges to watch *Mamma Mia!* for the 15th time, so know that the tips I'm giving have been tried and tested in the most extreme of circumstances. I'm talking, like, '*I can't be arsed to work, so instead I'm going to try and learn a dance routine to a Pussycat Dolls song*' levels of procrastination here. Over the years I've improved slightly, but it's still something that I have to actively work on; I apply the methods that I've detailed over the page almost daily.

I know I'm not the only one, though, and procrastination is the root of all evil in the workplace – aside from water-cooler gossip and the person who brings in cakes every week, which demonstrates our lack of willpower EVERY. SINGLE. TIME. It's the ultimate time-zapper; the reason why to-do lists remain unticked and a drain on any remaining shred of motivation. In order to stop it in its tracks, we must trick our brains into focusing and filtering out all distractions. Here are three practical methods to try when you feel procrastination creeping in:

CAN'T RESIST THE URGE TO SCROLL?

TIMED SCROLL SESSIONS

We all love a bit of a scroll. We can't deny it, and you know what? There's nothing wrong with it. Sometimes we need a break to rest, revive and gather up momentum to get going again. If taking a quick glance at your phone is an itch that you just need to scratch, then go ahead – but give yourself a time limit. Five minutes? 10 minutes? 15 minutes? Whatever you feel is necessary to satisfy your urge and act as an incentive to keep ploughing on. I'd recommend keeping it as short as possible so you don't have time to fall into a deep online shopping hole that's particularly painful to pull yourself out of. Next time your interest is waning, pick up your phone and set yourself an alarm to go off when it's time to get back on the horse. I swear by 10-minute breaks. It's enough time to read an article and have a quick flick through Instagram, but doesn't give you enough time to fully fall into the hole. Scroll, read, spin around on your chair – whatever – then jump back on once your time is up.

PERSONAL MATTERS THROWING YOUR CONCENTRATION GAME WAY OFF?

REGULAR BREAKS

In a similar vein to the previous method, I sometimes find that giving myself a defined break schedule works best. It sounds *way* more regimented than it actually is in practice, but I find that knowing when my next rest stop is keeps me on-task more effectively than if I was just taking a break when I felt I needed it (because that would be every 10 minutes – LOLZ). You might have heard of the 'Pomodoro' technique, which is to set a timer for 25 minutes, get your head down, then give yourself a five-minute break when the timer goes off, then repeat. Traditionally you'd do three to four 'Pomodoros' before you'd give yourself a longer break and you're ready to go again. Personally, I like to work for slightly longer stretches – anything from an hour to

90 minutes. Although feel free to modify – maybe it's working in short 10-minute bursts with a two-minute 'staring into space' break that might help you to actually tackle the battleground that is your inbox. I set a timer on my phone, put it in the other room so I'm not distracted, then attempt to get the task I've set myself completed without going off piste in my internet browser. It's the method that works best for me when my head is darting all around the place and I just can't seem to get settled. It forces me to focus, plus takes the procrastination magnet out of my gaze (aka my phone).

TRIED IT ALL AND STILL NOT CONCENTRATING?

LOCKED OUT
We're sort of amping up the strictness level as we go here, but if all else fails then it's time to pull out all the stops. If you need the temptation completely taken away then it might be worth looking into apps and programmes that allow you to restrict access to certain websites or just the internet completely. SelfControl and Cold Turkey both work on Macs to disable access to websites of your choice for a certain period of time; the former is free, and although the latter offers a free package too, the paid-for version allows you to give yourself daily time limits and even ties in 'Pomodoro'-style breaks. StayFocusd is a Google Chrome extension that allows you to create your own internet allowance for the day; once your time is up, you're locked out. One that works across all devices is Freedom, which blocks access to websites, the internet and apps. Although you do have to pay for the service, it's fully customisable to your needs and works across your computer and mobile. If it's your phone that's the issue then try the free Moment app that I've already mentioned back in the first section of the book; although it doesn't restrict any services, it does add up all your scrolling time, which can make for a gut-wrenching 'I'M NEVER GOING TO LOOK AT MY PHONE AGAIN' number come the end of the day.

The common denominator is that they all work to minimise distractions and keep you on-task for just a *little* longer. What we're aiming for is focus, which is the combination of being locked into an activity and having your mind free from any external factors that might turn your attention elsewhere. You're in the zone, your motivational levels are right up there, distractions right down there and everything is flowing. Speaking of which, you want to reach 'flow', the optimal state of productivity. Reach it and you'll get shit done at a rate you didn't even think was possible…

What is flow?

We have to cover *flow* in this chapter, because really it's the *dream* when it comes to productivity. You want the crib notes? Well, at its basic level it's the moment when you're completing a task and you're *in* it. You're feeling it, it's effortless and it's almost like instinct. Have you ever been so engrossed in what you're doing that you forget to eat and drink? Haven't been to the loo in about four hours? That's flow! When we're in the zone we lack awareness of our physical needs and time flies by without us even realising. Combine all these factors together and we have enhanced performance, we feel energised and we're actually enjoying what we're doing. TA-DAH! By entering this hyper-productive flow state the outcome is that we experience an increase in focused attention and we remain cool, calm, collected and unflappable about the task in hand. Sounds blissful, right?

The term 'flow' was first coined by the psychologist Mihaly Csikszentmihalyi, who noted this state of complete and utter productivity. You might be able to count those instances on one hand, or perhaps you find yourself there weekly; it can happen in a range of circumstances from education and sports and – more in the interests of an edited life – the workplace. It encapsulates everything that we've covered so far, by unpicking the perfect conditions under which optimum productivity is reached thanks to motivation riding high and distractions laying low. In order to unlock a flow state the task must have just the right balance of it being challenging and you feeling like you're extending yourself, while it also feels manageable and doable. The anticipation of accomplishment is what gets your motivation levels going. Then, seeing as we can only focus on a certain number of items at any time, when we enter flow we're using our complete focus on the task ahead, with minimal distractions. You see…

HIGH LEVELS OF MOTIVATION
+ MINIMAL DISTRACTIONS =
PRODUCTIVITY

WHY FLOW ROCKS:

- Focused attention and an increase in performance

- No feelings of stress or worry

- Timelessness

- Feeling energised and enjoying the task in hand

It sounds too good to be true, right? And that's partly correct, because realistically entering flow is only possible for tasks that tick off certain criteria. If we perceive the task as being too difficult for us or beyond our skillset then we instead enter a state of apathy and can experience anxiety because we feel the challenge is too high. So if it's a task you haven't completed before, isn't your strong point, or you're a bit confused by what you've been set, then there's a high chance that flow is off the cards. Counter to this, if we perceive the task as being too easy for us and below our skillset, then we enter a state of boredom and experience a lack of motivation, because we feel the challenge is too low. Maybe it's something that you do every day and you don't particularly enjoy; you feel like you've paid your dues when it comes to basic data entry and it's time for a fellow colleague to pick up that to-do-list task. You see? It's a tricky one to set up.

In order to access flow we must have a defined goal, clear objectives and be able to provide immediate feedback while we are in this mode. Often we might not have these factors available to us – when we're not sure of our defined role at work, have little communication and are unable to be 100% confident in our processes. So don't be too hard on yourself if flow seems like a stretch right now; instead read up on the steps to put it in place in the future, so reaching it becomes an option further down the line.

HOW DO WE TAP INTO FLOW?

If you're raring to go with a particular task, have motivation sweating out through your pores (that's you Mel!) or just have plenty of passion for whatever you're creating, then your energy is best used trying to get into a flow state ASAP. By reaching this productivity nirvana you're going to get what you need to get done faster and in the most effective and enjoyable way. Why wouldn't you want a one-way ticket there? Here are non-negotiables that need to be in place for a fast-track route to flow:

- We must know clearly what to do.

- We must know how to do it.

- We must be able to sense how well we're doing it.

- We must have freedom from distractions.

- We must perceive the challenge as high.

- We must perceive our skills as equally high.

These criteria also demonstrate how flow is not something that we can access with new tasks that have cropped up on our to-do list; it instead lends itself to processes that we've done many times before and can perform without really putting in too much thought. For me, editing a photo in some kind of fancy-schmancy software is still something I'm getting to grips with and learning, so flow isn't on the cards whenever that's in my schedule. However, I've written over 2,500 posts over my blogging career, and as it's a practised skill that I have that I've used over and over again, flow is a possibility. If you can draw this comparison in your own role, then here are the questions to ask yourself in order to get to that special place, as well as the troubleshooters to complete if you're not able to get there right now:

Do you clearly
know what to do?

Ask your manager for
further assistance or
research the task that
you need to complete

Do you know how
to do it?

Repeat the task as often
as possible so it becomes
learned and automatic

Are you able to sense how
well you're doing it?

Through repeating the
process you'll develop an
awareness of the quality
of your own work

Do you have freedom
from distractions?

Switch up your surroundings
and clear out your diary, so
you have a chance to focus

Do you perceive the
challenge as high?

See if there are any ways
you could advance the task
and go above and beyond

Do you perceive your
skills as equally high?

Save the flow process
for tasks you are set that
you feel are at the top end
of your ability

HELLO FLOW!

Once you get going, the chances are that the world around you will be on mute, but if you do start to hear the volume turning itself up, then do your best to eliminate distractions: work in a calm and quiet place if possible, and turn off all notifications and alerts. Of course you're going to have to come up for air occasionally, but if you feel flow take over then don't question it. Ride it out, and the chances are that you'll have one of the most productive few hours of your life so far. If you hit it once, you'll be able to access it even more easily next time, so practise if you can when the appropriate tasks come your way.

If it's not something that's coming easily to you, then don't fret. I mean, I've made a whole section about this here, and as you can see there's a lot of situational factors that have to be met in order for flow to say hello; just keep them in mind so you can attempt to apply them if the right to-do-list item ticks the boxes. Even if you're just trying to enter, you'll have set yourself up for a more efficient work session than you would have done otherwise. If not, and procrastination is still looming over you, following are some last-ditch-attempt techniques that I crack out whenever I'm in dire need of a kick up the rear, so I actually get *something* done...

How to up your productivity levels

If you've implemented everything that we've covered so far, then your productivity levels will have already shot up. FACT. So I'm going to keep this section pretty light, as really an increase in productivity is the end result of putting everything into practice, and with it all the other key beliefs that we want to fall into place: higher levels of motivation, more time spent doing what makes you happy, and therefore you living a more edited, streamlined and stress-free life. Basically, using your time in a way that serves you best, aka living an edited life.

Sometimes, in cases of extreme work fatigue when you really need to give yourself a kick up the arse, it's good to have some techniques to put into place when you're feeling like all your usual methods just aren't bringing the goods. So here are two practices that are easy to remember and can be whipped out when you feel like procrastination is a vacuum and it's sucking you in. Resist the pull with these two tricks:

THE 'ONE-TOUCH' RULE

DON'T BEGIN A TASK UNTIL YOU HAVE TIME TO SEE IT
THROUGH FROM START TO FINISH.

So you know that pile of unopened letters on your kitchen table? Instead of breaking down the task into little steps by opening them and then moving them to a spot to be dealt with later (gathering dust for a few weeks until you have to hurry home to update your road tax before it runs out because you forgot all about it), open up the letter, see you have road tax to pay, open up your laptop and settle the bill there and then.

If you're in a rush, then wait until you have a block of time where you'll be able to tackle whatever is inside the pile. It's a rigid framework so it doesn't work for everything – especially when it comes to longer projects – but it does work really well for paperwork and equally annoying errands, plus inboxes too. Don't open your inbox unless there's enough time on the clock for you to clear it. A good rule for those whose inbox was at zero this morning, but perhaps not the rule for you if your inbox count was 4,387 when you last checked.

THE 'THREE TASKS A DAY' RULE

SET YOURSELF THREE TASKS TO GET DONE TODAY.

It's one that I've tested and tweaked for years, but there is something magic about the number three. Not only is it the best number to write (in my personal opinion, although I'm partial to the number seven too), I've also found that completing three major tasks a day is a planning sweet spot for me. They easily slot into morning, lunchtime and afternoon timeframes and there's something about that number that feels like I've got just the right amount on my plate. It's not an amount that's going to leave me hungry for more, nor am I going to have to pop open my top button on my way home – it perfectly satiates my need for productivity, without leaving me feeling empty.

You might find that the number that lights a fire under your butt is higher or lower, so it's worth editing it to your own personal needs if three doesn't feel right. Have your own magic number tucked into your back pocket for use whenever you feel like your to-do list is making you want to vom. You could even go one step further by making sure that each of the three tasks falls into a different category, to add some variety to your day. Maybe make one project related, one admin and one creative?

See? I said I'd keep it light here. As practically 95% of the advice that I've put forward so far is ultimately to cut out time wasting, really you're a productivity pro by this point. Procrastination can take a hike, and if it's struggling to make its stage exit left, then at least now you have two ace cards up your sleeve to outsmart it.

The Edit

This final chapter of the work section of *An Edited Life* rounds things off nicely, I feel. Firstly we've tackled organisation. Your workspace should now be a functional area that's clean, tidy and free of paper piles. Hopefully your decluttering muscle has been strengthened and now you're ready for a slightly bigger task. Then we've focused on planning effectively: how to organise your day so that it fits you and your routines and habits best, plus how to structure lists so that they feel empowering and not overwhelming. Finally, we have moved on to ticking off those plans and how to actually get through your to-do lists. You're now chocker with new techniques that can be applied whenever you're next struggling with motivation, or when procrastination is setting up shop inside your brain. It's a three-pronged approach that covers all areas of organising and productivity in the workplace: setting up these plans in your new and improved working environment, and checking them off in a way that will give you an overall sense of achievement and the knowledge that you're getting shit done. You're doing the best job that you can, and hopefully you're doing it in a way that isn't increasing your stress levels and is allowing you breathing space in your non-working life, to spend more time doing as you please.

Congratulations! You're now two-thirds of the way through *An Edited Life*, which still means that you have one final section to get through where I see how many times I can get Ryan Gosling references into the narrative and convince you that life organisation is a fun and sexy topic. You've already got your life priorities in order, have beefed up your efficiency in your working hours, and now it's time to bring your newly honed streamlining skills back home...

AN EDITED WORK

WORK

CHECK LIST

- [ ] Declutter your workspace and supplies, and reorganise to create a functional area that's as comfortable and as free from distractions as possible.

- [ ] Through trial and error, find your best planning medium, whether that's putting pen to paper or downloading a scheduling app.

- [ ] Set yourself a realistic plan for the week ahead that makes you feel on top of things, instead of piling up your to-do list and increasing your feelings of anxiousness.

- [ ] Tidy up your inbox, and then once it's looking nice and neat, create your own rule that fits in best with you and your job, for how best to service it.

- [ ] Next time you're feeling highly motivated, note down five reasons why you think you're feeling that way so you can work on mustering up those ingredients next time it's lacking.

- [ ] If procrastination takes over, put one of the practical methods in place that I mentioned here: give yourself a timed break, download a website-restricting app or use the 'one-touch' rule.

HOME

Streamlining your home and editing your possessions is the final piece of the puzzle of an edited life. It's the step that pulls everything together. If your home is clean and tidy and doesn't look like it should be on an episode of *How Clean Is Your House?* then inviting friends over after work doesn't have to include an hour-long 'HIDE IT ALL!'/hoovering session before everyone turns up. Meal planning is a more pleasant experience if there isn't a month-old cauliflower in your vegetable drawer. Your Sunday self-care bath will actually happen if the tub isn't covered in last week's leg hair. A well-organised wardrobe can make getting to work on time in an outfit you actually quite like a possibility. It's the glue that holds the rest together, and by decluttering your home, you have less stuff to organise and an environment that should leave you feeling way more relaxed, and not like Kim and Aggie are going to knock down your door at any moment.

Get the bin bags out and get your comfies on, because the decluttering is about to begin. Say hello to your newly decluttered surroundings and prepare to get familiar with the fuss-free F.U.L.L. method.

Let's take away the urge for impulse shopping and solve the '*I don't have anything to wear!*' conundrum by creating a capsule wardrobe that's tailored to you and your needs. Learn why it's best to pick quality over quantity every single time (unless we're talking about doughnuts and a cleaning schedule). Finally we'll work out how to implement a cleaning and tidying routine to establish order and good habits into your home life.

So it's time for that final puzzle piece to create a space that's edited in order to make all aspects of your life and work as time-efficient and easy as possible, but in a way that still feels like you...

How to streamline and organise your home

Learn how to declutter your home using the F.U.L.L. technique, which is completely tailored to you so you're left with exactly what you need, use and love – nothing more, nothing less.

There's a high possibility that you picked up this book thinking that it was simply a decluttering manual, and I guess it is in some way. Throughout the chapters I've covered how to downsize and simplify all areas of life – from how to implement a regular digital detox into your routine, to how to write up a clear and concise plan that you'll actually see through to completion. I'm all for taking a minimalist approach across all aspects of everything that I do, but tweaking it in a way so that it doesn't feel restricting, and knowing that the process is a constant one that needs refining along the way – *hence the importance of editing*. It's full circle, baby! So while stripping back our possessions to a level that feels right for each and every one of us is part of the package, it plays into a wider framework here. From my experience, clearing out your home will not, as a sole action, change your life, but when combined with cogs from other areas like work and life moving in the right direction too – *then* it starts to get juicy.

Four years ago I delved headfirst into minimalist literature. I bought eight books on the matter (LOL! So ironic), searched online for resources and spent my free time listening to podcasts on the topic. During this period I was a real hoot to be around. As I mentioned in the introduction, I became a *wee* bit obsessed with tossing stuff out. Our home went from the show-home vibes that I pride myself on to looking like a discount furniture shop that was about to be shut down that afternoon. It was empty. My wardrobe was empty. The drawers were empty. And you know what? I felt empty too. I'd put so much energy and focus into removing as many material things from my life as was physically possible, that I'd completely disregarded the '*but maybe I need that?*' niggle that's sometimes right and sometimes wrong. I didn't have enough clothing to get through the week without needing to do two laundry loads, and our home was devoid of any personality (and almost of a remote control, but thankfully my common sense kicked in with that one). I thought when I'd completed my material shed that I'd feel unpinned and free – and I did for a short while. I thought I'd

levelled up to become some kind of minimalist guru. Marie Kondo
EAT YOUR HEART OUT. But then I started to smell myself because
I had to wear a shirt for the third day in a row, and I realised that I
might have taken things a little too far.

Of course there is the other end of the scale. Maybe Marie Kondo
has never crossed your mind and certainly never the contents of your
home? Perhaps you have a vase collection that rivals my mum's, or a
ticket stub collection that's bigger than my husband's and that regularly
explodes out of a drawer. If you love stuff and your surrounding clutter
brings you a happiness like no other, then good for you. However, if
you feel stifled and are regularly experiencing the negative effects or
inefficiencies that an overwhelming amount of possessions can bring,
then perhaps it's time to declutter. Here's the definition in terms of *An
Edited Life*…

DECLUTTERING: THE ACT OF CURATING A SPACE THAT SERVES YOU BEST, FILLING IT WITH THINGS THAT MAKE YOU HAPPY, NO MATTER THE AMOUNT, AND GETTING RID OF THE REST THAT DON'T.

Decluttering (or recluttering, if you've gone as minimalist as me) isn't
necessarily just about living with less. It's about living with what we
need, and a certain amount we probably don't need but that put a smile
on our face. My furry leopard print heels come to mind when I think
of the latter category – not necessary, but I feel absolutely banging
whenever I put them on. Our homes and the things that live inside
them shouldn't make us feel stressed; we have enough of that in the
outside world. So whether you identify as a hoarder or a minimalist,
or even if you're somewhere in the middle, a declutter is going to be
beneficial for you to edit your home to a place that best suits you, your
lifestyle and your square footage.

As with practically everything in life, streamlining your possessions is a
matter of moderation. I took it to the extreme and have since realised
that there's a place that sits slap bang in the middle, where we have

just the right amount of belongings. We've got what we need, we've got what we use, we love what we've got and the sight of them makes us feel good. We're not overwhelmed, nor under-served, and we have just the right number of clean shirts. There are an absolute shedload of techniques on offer when it comes to decluttering, but I'm going to tell you about one that's easy to remember, and should safeguard you from making the same mistakes that I did. *Leave that remote control alone!* Oh yeah, right – *erm*, it's just me that was eyeing that up…

The F.U.L.L. method

Some tidying strategies propose only holding onto things that give you joy. Others believe in a numbered approach – keep three jumpers, five pairs of shoes, one notepad and one holdall. Others set up a spatial restriction – everything you own must fit into a suitcase. I find the first theory to be a little vague, and the ones after that too militant; over recent years I've found the F.U.L.L. approach to work best. Never heard of it before? That's because I've made it up, but I've put it through the wringer, let me tell you, and it always leads to a logical decision when it comes to whether to give up an item or not. Here's what you need to ask yourself before you tackle each room and the accompanying belongings that are behind the door…

IS IT **FUNCTIONAL**? HAVE YOU GOT A USE FOR IT?
HAVE YOU **USED** IT IN THE LAST YEAR?
DO YOU **LOVE** IT?
DO YOU LIKE THE **LOOK** OF IT?

If your answer is yes to just one of these questions, then you keep it. And here's why it's foolproof…

The **functional** part means that you won't end up tossing away anything which could be useful. The question of when you last **used** it means that you won't end up hanging onto things that you haven't touched in years. By asking yourself if it's an item that you **love**, you're saving yourself the heartache of giving away anything that's sentimental or means a lot to you. Then, finally, sometimes you just have things that you like the **look** of and it's often these odd bits and trinkets that make your house feel like a home.

Compared with other approaches, this errs on the side of caution. From my experience I'd say that it's better to hold on to items that you're not sure you want to part with just yet, and sit on the decision for a while. If six months pass by and you still haven't **used** it and aren't finding yourself particularly attached either by its **look** or how it makes you **feel**, then you know what to do. As you build up confidence with decluttering and listening to your gut, then feel free to take it one step further. If you haven't worn an item in four years and you do love it, but actually you'd rather have the free hanger, then perhaps it's time to part ways. But don't worry – we'll work up to that.

The master declutter

Want to start? I'd suggest diving into the deep end and conducting a 'Master Declutter', where you give every room – and therefore everything you own – the F.U.L.L. treatment. This way you can be guaranteed to experience the full advantages across all aspects of your life that sprout from having an edited home environment. However, before you get started, make sure you have these things in place before you press go.

BEFORE YOU BEGIN

SET UP YOUR REMOVAL METHODS

Some items are no good for reuse so toss 'em in a big bag and wave goodbye. If you think you could make some dollar out of your old belongings, then set yourself up on a reselling website like eBay or Facebook Marketplace (Depop is good for clothing and Vestiaire Collective is the best place to sell designer goods) and have your account ready to go. Other things might not be worth selling, but friends and family might enjoy them, so I always like to keep a bag to the side to fill up and take with me next time I visit. Anything that is left over from my trips I take down to the charity shop. Think about fetes, stalls and charity sales that people you know run throughout the year and ask them if there's anything in particular they need for those. Waste not, want not, and all that; exhaust all avenues of passing on goods before you throw 'em in the bin and they're never to be seen again.

Unless you're already living in a white-walled cube that looks like a Bond villain's lair with just an artsy fireplace as the centrepiece, the chances are that if you plan on decluttering your home from top to bottom, then it's going to take a while. When you look at it as a whole it might seem daunting, so if that's the case break it up over a couple of weekends. That's how I best fit it in, while still clinging on to a basic level of human interaction and not turning into a bin-bag-obsessed thrower-outer. You need a bit of time on the clock and you need to actually want to do it (hopefully the rest of this chapter should put a fire in your belly). If you put in the hours here, you'll save them in the long run through owning a smaller amount of stuff which will make keeping them clean and tidy a shorter process. Plus by streamlining and counting up all the pounds you've wasted on these unwanted goods, it might help to shift your mindset away from buying things you don't need. So in the long run your budget benefits too. WIN-WIN.

THE MASTER DECLUTTER PLAN

When it comes to applying the F.U.L.L. method to your home I'd recommend that even the most seasoned streamliners among us should start small and work up to the bigger tasks. Along with breaking it down over a series of days or weekends if you're doing the whole caboodle, I'd suggest working on a room at a time. I must also warn you that about halfway through you may end up curling into the foetal position on the floor and wondering why the hell you began this never-ending task. So start with a room that's considered an easier task, like your bathroom – which contains a bit of product and just requires you to lob some empty shampoo bottles into the bin – then work up to the big boys like any storage space you own or your bedroom; places that hold your most prized belongings and a lot of them. That way by the time you've passed the halfway point, had your midway breakdown, picked yourself back up and you're racing to the finish line, your streamlining muscles will be well and truly pumped. You'll be deadlifting bags of paperwork, body-con dresses, threadbare socks and unwanted Christmas presents like a pro. I'd suggest going in this order:

1 Bathroom	**4** Kitchen
2 Hallway	**5** Bedroom
3 Living area	**6** Storage spaces

Here are some pointers to keep in mind when you're editing each room:

BATHROOM

I'd suggest ticking the easiest room off the list first, and for most I'm guessing that it's the bathroom. There isn't going to be much to declutter in there, unless you're like my old housemate who could have built a small fort out of the plastic razor guards that she left around the shower. I'll never forget the day that the plumber came round to unclog the drain and removed a clump of hair the size of a squirrel, along with a complex plastic structure of said razor guards.

DO:

- Only store items that are for hygiene and zen-inducing reasons.
- Keep everything tucked away in storage if possible, as it makes the area way quicker to clean.
- Stock all bathroom-related goods in there too, to save you having to nip across the hallway with your trousers round your ankles when you've run out of loo roll.

HALLWAY

The hallway is the entry point to your home and the first thing that you – and your guests – see when you walk through the door. Given that square footage is of a premium these days it can also find itself doubling up as a storage bunker/home office/general area that collates shit, and unless your hallway is absolutely chocker with covered storage, I'm here to campaign for materials in this space to be kept to an absolute

DO:

- Make sure that it smells good – you want it to feel inviting and smell like home (The White Company Fresh Fig Reed Diffuser is heaven).
- Keep it clear to avoid a tripping hazard as you try to bring the weekly food shop in.

minimum. In terms of practising what you preach, I feel like I should add here that our hallway is the current home of Mark's bike, cycling boots and all bike-related bumf (and he wants a second bike – FUN TIMES), so sometimes keeping it a junk-free spot isn't as easy as it sounds, but the less clutter, the better it is for your feng shui, or at least something like that...

LIVING AREA

Next, move on to your living area, which tends to be a bit different for everyone. Perhaps you have a dedicated living room, or you live in a studio space and just have an armchair and TV as your living space? Maybe you have an open-living area that flows straight into your kitchen? Whatever your scenario there really doesn't need to be that much material clutter in there. It's a space we use for chilling out in the evenings, hanging out at the weekends and socialising in our spare time; it's not really the area to dedicate to your lipstick collection or newly discovered love for beer-making and all the large and smelly appendices that come with it.

DO:

- Prioritise comfort with a sprinkling of interior personality.

- Keep the space clear and clutter-free so there's more room for you to stretch out and enjoy your *Great British Bake Off* obsession in peace, with a gigantic slice of shop-bought Victoria sponge.

KITCHEN

Ok, here's where things really start to heat up. In order to reach the calming upper echelons of *An Edited Life*, we need our kitchens to be the most fully functioning area of our homes. We need them to be clean. We need

DO:

- Create a functional and clean space to store fresh goods.

- Find storage hacks for your pantry essentials to keep them well organised.

- Make sure that all kitchen utensils are easy to reach when you need them.

them to be tidy. We need them to be organised in such a way that we don't forget about the smoked garlic bulb that our sister brought us back from France which started to honk so bad that we thought that a rat had died in the back of our cupboards. If the F.U.L.L. method isn't applied, then the chances are that meal planning will be a distant dream as you desperately try to jam open a freezer drawer to fish out an old sausage that's been rolling around in there for a paltry dinner substitute.

BEDROOM

You know the whole 'your bedroom is your oasis' thing? Well I am fully on board with that. Your bedroom should be the top spot in your home that elicits feelings of rest and relaxation by the bucketload. A space for stress to take a back seat and for you to be able to recharge your batteries back up to their full potential with minimal distractions, physical or mental. For a lot of us,

DO:

- Reserve the room for sleeping antics only and avoid using it as a multi-functional space where possible.

- Store clothing in a way that's neat and tidy and keeps it in good nick - in other words, not on your floor.

though, it's a high-traffic storage spot so we need to learn how to use it efficiently, while still creating an area that's free from clutter. Let's find the balance between streamlining, storage and sleep...

STORAGE SPACES

Christmas decorations, suitcases, extra tins of paint, the picture of Charlie Simpson that you drew for your year nine art project and deem one of your best works – we've each got our own manifestations of things we need but not on a daily basis, and things that we just can't bring ourselves to get rid of. I'm betting that they live in your additional storage space, if you've been blessed with an extra nook or cranny in your home. Whether you have an airing cupboard-cum-storage spot or a whole loft to yourself, there's something about having this extra space that means that it's a dead-cert to be filled to maximum capacity. Heck, even Monica Geller had a cupboard brimming with things! The first step is to GET IT OUT. Give it the F.U.L.L. once-over and then return what's left into your storage area in a way that screams organisation and will hopefully stop it turning back into an overflowing volcano of stuff you need, but don't actually need that often anytime soon.

DO:

- Get everything out – don't hold back. You need to give every single item in your home the F.U.L.L. treatment – no exceptions.

- Invest in storage solutions where needed in order to keep things packed in a way where it's easy to find them and stop them from being damaged.

You've set up your removal methods, you've got time on your side, you've got an idea of the end goal of each room thanks to the previous section and you're all systems go. Next are your crib sheets for each room in your home; starting with the F.U.L.L. method and some suggestions for what you might find in each category that will help you efficiently declutter your things. Then following with organisation tips for how to re-home what remains in order to make each room as streamlined and functional as possible.

Bathroom

F: TOWELS, FLANNELS, HYGIENIC GOODS
(TOOTHPASTE, SHOWER GELS, SHAMPOO, TOILET
ROLL ETC) AND BATHROOM CLEANING SUPPLIES

U: ADDITIONAL SKINCARE, BODY AND HAIR ITEMS

L: PLANTS AND CANDLES

L: FANCY HAND SOAP AND MOISTURISER DISPENSERS
AND AESTHETICALLY PLEASING STORAGE

BEAUTY PRODUCTS. Keep whatever you can stored away. It not only keeps everything fresh, but it also makes cleaning the bathroom a dream. IKEA do fab bathroom cabinets at a decent price. If you ever have a chance to renovate a bathroom then I highly recommend buying a sink unit with storage. Buy plastic bins to keep each occupant's shower and bath goods in, removing it from the storage drawer when you need it and retuning it afterwards; aiming to never have shampoo bottles and shower gels around the bath/shower. It gets grim, it's difficult to clean and any in-shower storage turns to pure mould in about two months.

HYGIENIC GOODS. This is the first bathroom we've had where there has been storage for toilet rolls within an arm's reach of the loo and it's a small but significant nugget of design that I'm over the moon about. Loo sprays, toilet rolls, sanitary products, cleaning products; store them in the bathroom if there's space, so everything is ready and waiting in the bathroom-zone when you need it.

TOWELS. If stored in a drawer I find it best to roll them to save on space and so I can see them all at a glance, but however they're kept always put back your fresh towels at the bottom of the pile and take from the top, so you're getting equal use from them all. As a general rule of thumb I'd say that three towels per person is a good number, plus one for gym/beach use; remove any that have seen better days or are from the eighties and haven't dated well.

Hallway

F: COAT STAND, KEY DISH AND A PAPERWORK
STAND

U: (NOT NECESSARILY AN APPLICABLE TOOL TO USE
IN THE HALLWAY)

L: PRINTS AND FRAMED PHOTOGRAPHS

L: DECORATIVE ITEMS (VASES, PLANTS, CANDLES,
REED DIFFUSERS ETC)

SHOES & COATS. We had a coat cupboard under the stairs when we were growing up, so keeping our coats, jackets and shoes in there made complete sense. However, every place that I've lived since doesn't have this handy storage nook. If there's a dedicated space for all your outerwear then make use of it, but if not I'd recommend keeping them in your wardrobe instead. Struggling to open your front door because of the bundle of coats behind it, or a shoe pile that's fashioned itself into an unmoveable wedge just ain't chic. Edit them down if required and then find an alternative place to store them out of sight that way your hallway won't be confused with the entry point to Narnia.

PAPERWORK. Your hallway is not a substitute for an office filing system, so don't treat it like one as, trust me, unpaid bills aren't the first thing you want to be greeted with when you open the door. I'd recommend opening post as soon as you receive it, actioning as much as you can ASAP and then if there are things that need to be actioned at a later date, to keep them in a high-traffic area so you are constantly reminded that they need to be completed. For most of us that's either going to be the hallway or the kitchen, so if you are going to dump your life admin in your hall I'd recommend at least getting a little letter holder to store it in or putting up a paperwork basket onto the wall (H&M and Etsy do nice ones), so it's a bit more visually appealing, but still flicks the 'THIS NEEDS TO BE SORTED SOON' switch in your brain.

BOOKS. The F.U.L.L. method works especially well here and is what I adopt when it comes to my bookcase. I only keep hold of books that provide a function (recipe books, or books that I find helpful in my job), books that I refer back to often (I read out the hen party chapter of Dolly Alderton's *Everything I Know About Love* to every person who enters our home), books that I love and ones that I like the look of, because sometimes a coffee table book is just pleasing to the eye. Books that don't fall into any of these four categories are passed on and donated once I've read them, so this way our living room doesn't turn into a library of exclusively fashion, beauty, chick-lit and life organisation books.

RECORDS/DVDS/BOARD GAMES. I am one of those terrible people who just prefers everything to be digitalised (aside from books – I've yet to jump on the Kindle wagon, although I accept that it does make sense for travel). So if it was up to me we'd own a small collection of records and no CDs and DVDs. Seeing as everything is so easy to store on your various different devices and up in the clouds these days I'd say hold onto the category of items that you actually use, or those that have sentimental value to you. If you crack out your *Love Actually* DVD yearly, then keep it. Have a record that you enjoy playing from beginning to end a couple of times a year? Keep it somewhere safe. But for everything else it's time to donate - including that Scrabble set that you've never used. A shelving unit that has a mixture of open and closed shelves is a godsend because it means that you can store all your non-visually pleasing crap, along with the stuff that it's nice to have out on display too.

Kitchen

F: ALL KITCHENWARE, DINNERWARE, CUTLERY AND
UTENSILS

U: FOOD

L: RECIPE BOOKS AND CROCKERY PASSED DOWN
FROM FAMILY MEMBERS WITH SENTIMENTAL VALUE

L: ANY KITCHEN GADGETRY FUN TO KEEP
STORAGE INCIDENTALS WITH KEY TABLE RUNNERS,
COASTERS AND MATS

FRIDGE FOODS. Keep gas-releasing fruit and veg out of the fridge as it can spoil other veggies prematurely. So pop your avocados, bananas, nectarines, peaches, pears, plums and tomatoes in a bowl on the side or stored away in a cupboard. But for the fridge here's the best map to follow:

UPPER SHELVES: Store foods up there that don't require cooking; like leftovers, cooked meats and drinks.

MIDDLE SHELVES: Pop all your dairy goods here – milks, yoghurt, cheeses and butter.

LOWER SHELVES: As this is the coldest part of your fridge, store all your uncooked meats and fish on the lower shelves, making sure that everything's well covered and sealed.

BOTTOM DRAWER: The perfect place for loose fruits and veggies and bags of salad.

DOOR SHELVES: These are the warmest part of the fridge and subject to the most fluctuations in temperature, so keep foods with natural preservatives in the door shelves like juices, jams, spreads and condiments.

FREEZER FOODS. Ditch anything that's been in there for over six months (after that things tend to lose their flavour), then organise the remaining goods by category into each drawer. We have three drawers, so I use the top one for frozen veg, bread, fish and meat, the middle one for leftovers because it's the largest and that's what we have most of, and then the bottom one which is the smallest for sweet things like ice cream and frozen fruit. When it comes to leftovers, make sure you're storing them in useable size portions, in clear containers or bags if possible and label each one so you know what's inside and when you froze it (or leave off the label if you like to play the age-old game of 'leftover lotto' and wish to have a surprise for dinner).

PANTRY GOODS. Store lesser-used goods up high and things that you need access to most days on lower shelves. You know those lazy susan spinny-round-things? Not only are they really fun to play with, but they're also a great way to store spices and tinned goods. For what you lose in space, you gain in easy retrieval. Transparent baskets are really handy too for storing things like flours, grains, nuts and dried fruit that can be grouped together which makes them easier to find. Kilner jars are the preferred storage method on Pinterest and if you're looking to reach organisation nirvana then be my guest and go nuts with your label maker; but bear in mind that they require a bit of time to arrange and upkeep, so don't feel like a failure if your flour remains in its original bag.

PLATES, POTS, PANS & EVERYTHING ELSE. When you're putting all your kitchen goods back, store things close to where they are used; cookware and utensils by the oven, dishware by the dishwasher etc etc. Stacking is the devil and makes removing items a back twinge just waiting to happen, so adjust your inner-cupboard shelving to the optimal height to fit everything in and cabinet risers are a great idea if you're short on space (little mini stands that you can put in your cabinets to create an extra shelf). If ever you find yourself re-doing a kitchen, install as many drawer units as possible because it makes storing and sorting things like your plates, pans and Tupperware boxes a BREEZE. Worth the price of a new kitchen just for those alone (I wish I was joking, but I'm not).

Bedroom

F: FURNITURE AND A VANITY SET-UP
U: CLOTHING, SHOES, ACCESSORIES, MAKEUP, BEAUTY
ITEMS, BEDDING, BOOKS AND CHARGERS
L: SLEEP SPRAYS AND SENTIMENTAL OBJECTS
L: PRINTS AND PHOTOS, PLANTS, A MIRROR AND A WELL-
ORGANISED BEDSIDE TABLE

CLOTHING, SHOES & ACCESSORIES. This is a topic
covered in the next chapter thanks to a deep dive into
capsule wardrobes. I utilise my clothing best when it's all
hung up. Under-bed storage works well for out-of-season
clothing and using transparent bins on the top shelves
of a wardrobe that are difficult to reach, instead of piling
up clothing means that you don't end up with jumpers
cascading down onto your head every time you try and
dislodge the one from the bottom of the pile.

BEDSIDE TABLE. A quick scan of my husband's side
of the bed uncovers a museum ticket from six months
ago, Euros, three months of his engineering magazine
subscription still in the plastic wrapping, five lip balms,
two watches and a Woodland Trust leaf identification
swatch book. Now I get it, if you don't have office space in
the home then sometimes you just need space to put *stuff*
temporarily, you know? I'd argue that the bedroom isn't
this spot (the kitchen or hallway is much better suited)
and about 50% of these items could probably be tossed.

BEAUTY BITS. The majority of our makeup is going to
reside in our bedrooms (unless you find yourself as an
accidental beauty blogger and therefore keep makeup in
your bedroom, office AND bathroom). I like to keep things
tucked away if possible and close to where I use them. I
have a MUJI mini plastic set of drawers for my everyday
makeup out and I keep my hairdryer and all styling tools
away in a drawer. A small, but significant step that makes
my morning routine even quicker.

Storage spaces

I'm forgoing the F.U.L.L. recommendations here, because our storage spaces are crammed with weird and wonderful things. Instead, complete the F.U.L.L. analysis of whatever you find in there, re-use and re-home whatever you can before getting rid of the rest. Here's how to store the remaining items away...

STORAGE FOR LARGE AREAS: When storing items in bigger storage spaces, transparent plastic storage bins are LIFE. You can see what's inside them and everything will stay clean and safe as they are sealed and waterproof. They also stack and they're nice and light.

STORAGE FOR ITEMS OFTEN NEEDED: Keep items that you use often at the front of your cupboard or by the loft hatch, so you don't have to dig around the depths. Just like your pantry, keep your most-used things low and at the front and items you use the least high up and at the back.

BE SELFISH WITH YOUR SPACE: Now I'm not suggesting that you be a class A knob when it comes to this, but if you do have oodles of storage space, I wouldn't go broadcasting this around as there's a high chance that you'll become the Big Yellow Self Storage Company of your friends. We have a large loft area and when we moved in we became part-time furniture storers for our friends and family. Three years later when we were having a tidy-out it turns out that everyone had completely forgotten what was up there and wanted us to donate it to the local charity shop. Of course if there's someone who needs a short-term solution then step up.

CHECK-IN BI-YEARLY: Like coffee cups, items that we keep in dedicated storage spaces seem to procreate whenever we look away, so I'd recommend scheduling in a twice-yearly tidy-up. It's not necessary to do an extreme streamline of all your packed-away goods every time, but more just to perform a quick audit of what you've got; see if there is anything that you can remove and pass on and just to make sure that it's all neat, clean and still in good condition up there.

This book could double up as a PhD thesis if I went into the exact steps that I'd suggest for every single possible item that someone could own, but hopefully I have given you some ideas for how to deal with the areas of your home that are typically the most congested. From your bathroom to your storage space, you've given everything the F.U.L.L. treatment, and found organisation methods that work for your space, but what do you do when it comes to your 'shit drawer' and the stuff that falls into the first 'L' category: that you love and that pull on your heartstrings? Here's how to tackle those two tough areas...

How to organise the 'shit drawer'

Every house has a shit drawer. Sometimes it resides in the hallway. Other times it might hide away in the bedroom. However, for us, it's always been in the kitchen. You know the drawer that you have to tease with much tugging back and forth because something's got wedged in there, and then when it jolts open screws, sellotape, paracetamol, unused IKEA allen keys and takeaway menus from the tandoori down the road that you haven't ordered from in four years, all fly out? Yeah, that. Here's how to turn it into a drawer that actually opens, in four easy steps:

1   Firstly, give every item the F.U.L.L. treatment – I can pretty much guarantee that about 80% of it can be binned. No one needs that many half-used birthday cake candles.

2   Shit drawers aren't best suited to being one big drawer as they're difficult to organise. Instead, clear out some cupboard space and invest in a stacking acrylic drawer system (MUJI do some fab ones).

3   Categorise the shit and split between how many drawers you have. That way it's easy to find what you need.

4   If you want to go one step further get yourself a label maker (I bought the Dymo Omega Home Embossing Label Maker) and label the relevant drawers. We have 'medicines', 'stationery' and 'tool bits'. Your shit drawer will be the most visually organised area of your kitchen.

What to do about the sentimental stuff

I'll make sure I shout this loud enough for the people at the back, but just because you fancy borrowing some principles from a minimalist lifestyle or trying a more streamlined approach on for size, it does not mean that you're *not* allowed to hold on to sentimental things. I repeat: SENTIMENTAL THINGS ARE A-OK! Trinkets, photos and hand-me-downs are part of our make-up, and can play a really important role in any bereavements and memories you have experienced. We're either sentimental or we're not, and if you're the latter, well then good for you – you probably have spare storage space coming out of your earholes and this chapter has been an absolute breeze for you. But if you enjoy poring over photos and just can't imagine ever tossing your nan's brooch in a charity bag *gasps* then that doesn't make you any less of *An Edited Life* adopter.

I can shred through a wardrobe of clothing with the speed of a chainsaw, but when it comes to all the sentimental shit I'm a complete and utter sap. I love nothing more than looking through old tickets, stubs and Polaroids, and still have every single note, card or letter that Mark has ever given me. I have the Topshop dresses that I wore on my 18th birthday, my 21st birthday and my graduation. I have all the photos that I printed out and stuck on my wall at uni which I thought made me look really cool and artsy, and I regularly check in round my grandparents' house to have a root around their chronologically organised photo album collection. Old stuff is lovely! It's nostalgic! It flickers memories back to life! They are storytelling tools, and if you want to keep something that puts a smile on your face or brings back the thought of something or someone that was close to your heart, then hold it tight and keep it well away from the bin-bag black hole.

Here's the only rule that I'd give you. If you're going to keep the sentimental stuff then at least enjoy it. Now, I'm not recommending that you open some kind of personal relic museum here because that would be WEIRD and a red flag to any guests and possible acquaintances entering your home, but if there's a way of organising these belongings so that they're displayed and therefore easier to enjoy, then do it.

Of course, with photos it's easy. Buy yourself some albums, edit and pick out the ones that you really want to keep to look back on and arrange them accordingly. I really enjoy doing this and arm myself with Paperchase albums and a label maker, and have a whale of a time. We once did a mammoth session that took us days to complete where we went though every single photo that we owned and created photo albums with our favourites, but now I make it my personal mission to print out any films and pictures we've taken on our phones after any trips or visits away and get them in an album ASAP. I find that Snapfish do a good job of printing pictures quickly and not at a price that makes you never want to print another picture ever again. The original organisation sesh might have taken a while, but keeping on top of it from that point onwards means that the upkeep isn't as much of a time drain and you end up with some cracking albums that you can browse whenever you fancy. If your future grandchildren are anything like me, they'll be grateful of your efforts.

Photos are an easy one to organise, but what about things that you can wear, or play with, or actually use? I'm thinking jewellery, clothing, tools, kitchenware, books. Stuff that warms your cockles, but which – unless you actually bring them out to see the light of day – will remain in that box with the writing on the side that you can't really decipher: 'GRANDMA'S BITS'? 'BOBS?', 'BUTTS!??'. Some items aren't fit for everyday use. Take, for example, my Topshop dresses that are an act of pure entertainment whenever I try to fit into them, with there now being too much sausagemeat to fit into the sausage skin, no matter how much sucking in I do. They are destined for a life in a box in the loft, only ever to be removed after I've had a bit too much to drink and think that then is the *perfect* time to try and squeeze them on, or if I am ever blessed with a daughter who will probably think they are godawful and wouldn't touch them with a bargepole anyway. I find both of these scenarios hilarious and will hold on to the three dresses for these two reasons alone. However, for our wedding, my grandparents gave us an old jug and glass set from the sixties which looks so flippin' cool and so flippin' breakable. Instead of wrapping it in newspaper and popping it up in the hole in the roof, we've used it. Nuts, I know. We have it in our cupboard and we use it whenever we have a gin, or a cocktail, or a summer drink of some kind. We're now down to five glasses as there was a bit of an *incident*, but that's alright. They're retro and fun, they make me think of my grandparents whenever I use them, and I'm sure they love that. So take anything out of storage that could be put to use in some way: clean, tailor, repair, re-size, re-sharpen where necessary, and get it back in action.

Some items are there to be read, or flicked through, or just held. If they're stick-able then treat yourself to a scrapbook and fashion yourself a sentimental page-turner that gives you all the feels whenever you take the time to have a read-through (top tip: keep it on your bookshelf so you can access it easily). If it's not really scrapbook material, then keep it in a box with the rest of your sentimental stuff. Label it accordingly (on all sides of the box), make sure that it's stored securely and is safe from any water damage, and try to check in with it each time you pop into your storage space so it doesn't sit there unloved.

The moral of the story here is that if you're going to hold on to something that would feel gut-wrenching to lose, then find a way to use it. Re-size your nan's ring and wear it. Enjoy these items for what they are and remind you of, let your eyes get a bit weepy, dab 'em dry and then be on your merry way. Keep what you love, ditch what you don't and edit your sentimental stash into a personalised memory bank, just for you.

The Edit

Streamlining and organising our home and belongings is the classic 'getting my shit in order' step, and it's easy to see why. For most of us the feeling of shedding stuff is a cathartic one and we end up dialling down the stress-o-meter a couple of notches because of it. Our homes are filled with less clutter, our minds feel less cluttered because of it and we're able to make time-efficient changes left, right and centre because of it. Cleaning, organisation, tidying, meal planning, even getting ready in the morning: they can all be sped up if we streamline our material things. It's impossible to tell you what I'd recommend doing with each and every item that you own, but I hope this chapter has taught you the F.U.L.L. framework that can be applied in every room of your home, and given you some storage ideas. The end result will I hope leave you at a place where your home feels like a home (just a slightly more organised one), gives you all the chill vibes when you step inside and doesn't require so much upkeep. Less stuff = less to keep tidy. I mean, *that's* motivation to streamline right there.

I have only brushed over it in this chapter, but I would *highly*, highly recommend organising your clothing in accordance with capsule wardrobe principles. I know I sound like a broken record (I've been harping on about it on my YouTube channel for the past four years), but adopting a capsule wardrobe has decreased the amount I shop, the time I spend pondering what to wear in the mornings and the cost-per-wear of the items that I own. A saver of money AND time? Need more convincing? I have a whole chapter ahead to twist your arm...

How to build a capsule wardrobe

Edit your wardrobe into a well-maintained, high-quality seasonal capsule that will not only save you time getting ready in the morning, but will dial back your spending in your budget too.

If I asked the question, 'What area of your home do you feel like you need to streamline the most?', I'm guessing that around 80% of you would say your bulging wardrobe, and that's why I'm giving it a whole chapter of its own. Since I adopted the capsule wardrobe philosophy four years ago, it's had an impact that's stretched further than just clothing. I now shop in a more conscious way across all products. I no longer waste half as much time browsing online and committing every item that ASOS sells to memory. I now very rarely make impulse purchases (hey – *I'm still human!*) and am able to spot the high-quality items that I know I'll still be wearing in 10 years' time that are worth the investment. More importantly, I save money and am able to organise my clothing in the small closet space that I have, in a way that means I can easily see everything that I own and don't have to do a Lady Gaga-esque speedy outfit change five times before I leave the house in the morning. It might seem like a minute detail, but the effect of editing your clothing selection trickles down and can have significant financial and time-saving gains.

If you have to wrestle with your wardrobe to unhook the dress you want to wear for the day or your vest top pile in your drawer looks like a big bowl of spaghetti, then the concept of a capsule wardrobe might sound a little daunting to you. The phrase 'capsule wardrobe' itself has been bandied around for *years*. It's a Fashion Editor favourite to dictate the 10 items you need to create the ultimate Parisian-flavoured edit (and, yes, of course I lap it up every time the concept's recycled) and if you type it into YouTube over 200,000 videos are uploaded on the matter, with a fair few featuring yours truly. A further search on Pinterest uncovers a whole wealth of pictures of chic-looking clothing, hung out with perfectly finger-measured spaces between them, on a rail in a room that looks like it's taken right from the pages of *Architectural Digest*, which might not do much to humanise the idea. But take a moment – is your answer 'yes' to any of the following questions:

- Do you struggle to find what you want to wear in the mornings because your wardrobe is so full?

- Do you feel stressed because there's just so much in there that you're indecisive about what you want to wear?

- Do you find yourself wearing an item just a handful of times before you fall out of love with it or forget about it?

- Do you spend more hours than you wish to admit browsing the 'What's New' sections of your favourite online shops?

If your answer is yes to even just one of the above, then it's time to get serious about the idea of a capsule wardrobe. Let me tell you a little secret: it's not that hard. Literally anyone can master the art of the perfect clothing edit, whether you're starting the process with 10 pairs of shoes or a 100. There are many methodologies out there, but over the years I've honed a technique which is not restrictive and allows you to retain all the advantages of a capsule wardrobe, and to find your style while still being able to have fun and go balls out on & Other Stories from time to time. It's not about rules, or strictly owning a certain number of items; it's about learning what works for you and your needs and ultimately saving time and money while you're at it – and who doesn't want that?

The idea is simple. With the turn of each season, your wardrobe will be re-jigged and re-evaluated. As the weather turns it will be time for you to:

- Empty out your wardrobe

- Re-hang any items that are still suitable

- Put the rest that aren't into storage

- Add clothing back into your wardrobe that had previously been in storage and is now just right for the upcoming season

This editing process leaves you with a mix of year-round staples and a fresh crop of clothing for spring, summer, autumn and winter, meaning that your summer dress stash isn't getting in the way during the winter when you just want to be able to get at your parka jacket. Instead, your knee-skimming numbers will be in storage ready for the sun to make an appearance again next year, with your big jackets that give Liam Gallagher a run for his money hanging up in pride of place in your wardrobe.

Creating this seasonal capsule means that you're only ever looking at clothing that's suitable for the three months ahead, making it easier to select items and easier to organise. Keeping a narrow assortment of clothing will also help to decrease decision fatigue. You know when there's so much to choose from that it's stressful to come to a final decision, and nine times out of ten you make the wrong one because there were just so many options? A capsule wardrobe, along with your newly streamlined possessions, thanks to the tips from the previous chapter, can help to alleviate this mind clutter.

One thing that we can all be pretty useless with at times is the re-wearing of clothes and recycling of items from past seasons. We're all tuned in to the magpie mindset of constantly wanting new, shiny things. The idea of dusting off a jumper for the forthcoming winter that you purchased three years ago just isn't as appealing as buying that fluffy, soft number that you brushed past in Topshop the other day – a scene that was lifted right out of a romcom. We've all been there. But the concept of having a wardrobe that shifts seasonally every three months means that with a couple of purchases at the beginning of each rotation to replace old items that have seen better days, or that cater to a particular trend that you're into, you'll end up giving wear-time to everything in your wardrobe. It forces you to do a clothing inventory four times a year, which I promise is more exciting than it sounds. No longer will you end up re-buying a scarf every year because you've completely forgotten about the one that you bought the year before that, *and the one from the year before that.* When it comes to occasions like weddings or parties, you'll have a small edit of pieces that you can mix and match with different accessories, and so not have to panic-purchase 15 dresses off ASOS the night before. With a handful of clever investments each season, you'll feel the bee's knees in your old buys.

Within the context of an edited life, possibly one of the best capsule wardrobe wins comes from the fact that it's one less string in your procrastination bow. Sure, the string for videos of cats high-fiving their owners is still there, and a day without browsing through a 'You'll Remember This if You Were a Kid in the Nineties' article is just plain wrong, but the hour-long 'What's New' scrolling sessions will become a thing of the past. When I began totalling up the amount of time that I spent drooling over the pages of my favourite fashion haunts online, and making imaginary baskets that accumulated to a deposit for a house, it wasn't a figure that filled me with joy. Why wasn't I doing something useful? I could have been learning a second language! Learning to knit! Finally got around to defrosting the freezer, which is something I've had on my to-do list for the past two years! Let's just say when you get to the point that you have a favourite ASOS model, you know that something's got to change.

How to build a capsule wardrobe

Over the years that I've managed a capsule wardrobe, I've done it all. I've owned a minuscule amount of clothing, I've made impulse purchases (although decidedly fewer than I would have had I not been in experiment mode), I've bought things that five years later are still absolute staples in my wardrobe, and I've made investments that were utterly terrible and ultimately bad decisions (the Saint Laurent sandals that made my feet bleed for days were a low point).

Now, I'm not saying that the act of firstly streamlining your current wardrobe situation and then employing a capsule wardrobe methodology will transform you into the owner of a perfectly formed closet immediately. The process takes time, but a couple of years down the line you'll end up with something pretty special. By then you'll have built up your basics, will be able to more intuitively decide whether a garment is worth the investment or not, and will have worked out just the right amount of clothing that feels like it gives you options, but doesn't feel overwhelming.

Ready? Let's do this!

STEP ONE: GET IT ALL OUT

I'm a big fan of the 'getting it all out' method when it comes to tidying. Having all your belongings from one genre grouped together in a massive pile should spur you on to downsize, and it means that once you've started you're committed, unless you fancy spending the next week wading through your clothing just to exit the bedroom.

1. Empty out the contents of your wardrobe onto a clear space where it will be easy to sort.

2. Do this step after you've done a big wash and you're able to get 95% of all the clothes and shoes that you own in one place.

3. Leave all other clothing groups out of it for now – accessories, pyjamas, activewear etc. – so it doesn't get too unbearable.

4. Give your wardrobe and drawers a good scrub while they're temporarily empty.

STEP TWO: CREATE PILES

It's a tad stressful to just stop and stare at this clothing volcano that you've created in the middle of your bedroom, so DON'T DO IT – keep moving.

1. Sort through everything and make piles:

   - One for things that you haven't worn in the past year and are happy to donate and pass on (I sometimes extend this to 18 months, because often there are some items of clothing that I only ever wear on hot-weather holidays or if the UK becomes a furnace).

- One for things that need to be cleaned, repaired or altered.

- One for items that are a hard 'HELL YEAH' that you wear often, that fit well and work with your style.

2 Act on these piles, although if you're struggling to part with certain things, do the 'out of sight, out of mind' trick, by bundling them into a bin bag and hiding them somewhere in your home. Set a reminder to dig them out in a couple of months' time, and if you still feel the same way then keep them, and if you didn't miss them at all then it's time for them to go to a better home.

STEP THREE: SEASONALISE AND ORGANISE

I'm completely making up a word here, but I feel like you get the gist.

1 From the pile of items that you wear often and you're keeping, split it into two:

- One pile for items that are unsuitable to wear in the current season and need to go into storage.

- Another pile for items that you're currently wearing. TA-DAH – there you have yourself a capsule wardrobe!

2 Roll up and store your out-of-season clothing and get hanging your current items. Keep an eye out later in the chapter when I share how best to organise it all in the most efficient, yet swoony way.

STEP FOUR: GIVE IT SOME TIME

So your capsule wardrobe has arrived. It's hanging in your wardrobe
and you're feeling like a BOSS. You have a slightly smaller pool of
clothing to pick from and you've kept your mitts away from Zara for
longer than 24 hours. Well done. At this point it's tempting to jump
back into the shopping cycle, but I'd highly recommend pressing pause
and taking a break.

1   Spend two weeks to a month testing out your capsule and
working out what you need more of, what you need less
of, if there's anything that's missing – get to know it.

2   Keep notes and make a list whenever you think of
something that you'd like to purchase, to assist you next
time you're out shopping, either in a page in your Bullet
Journal or organisation software or notebook. These days
I don't go shopping without knowing what gaps in my
wardrobe need filling. It's completely cool to expand from
time to time (I usually make purchases at the beginning of
each new season and then try to abstain for the rest of the
period), but do it mindfully.

STEP FIVE: TIME FOR A CHANGE

For me the cyclic repetition of capsule wardrobes is the best bit. Just as
your interest starts to wane in your current clothing set-up, it's time to
re-load with your old favourites, sprinkle in a few new items that you
were missing, if required, and go again for another 12 weeks – which
always completely zips by. The act of constantly shopping your own
stash adds some excitement to the whole thing and spurs you on just as
you were reaching that '*I have stuff to wear, but I'm so bored of wearing it*'
phase.

How you break your capsule wardrobe down seasonally is going to be
different depending on what hemisphere you call home. However,
I've detailed my set-up below. I'd suggest testing it out in three-month
chunks first so you're following these steps four times a year.

- Try to schedule in a bit of wardrobe time on the first weekend of each new season, and pop a reminder in your diary.

- On that day, take everything out of your wardrobe and do the three-pile split from Step Two again ('definitely keep' items, pieces that need dry cleaning, alterations or repairs, and items to donate). Sort through the 'definitely keep' items, hanging seasonally appropriate items back in your wardrobe and putting the rest into storage. Then go through your previously stored items, putting things back into your wardrobe that will be perfect to wear for the upcoming season.

MY CAPSULE WARDROBE SCHEDULE

Some seasons I feel the need to update my capsule more than others. The beginning of summer and winter mark the biggest shifts in weather, so those re-dos always tend to be more impactful than the ones that I do for spring and autumn, and if I feel like skipping a season because I'm happy with exactly what I own, that's cool too. There's flexibility in a capsule wardrobe set-up, you just have to tweak it for yourself. Mid-season and you fancy buying a coat? BE MY GUEST.

SPRING CAPSULE:
March, April & May – small update

SUMMER CAPSULE:
June, July & August – bigger update

AUTUMN CAPSULE:
September, October & November – small update

WINTER CAPSULE:
December, January & February – bigger update

WHAT TO DO WITH YOUR OTHER ITEMS

So your wardrobe is looking like you've worked some serious streamlining magic, but what do you do with all the other bits and bobs that you have hanging around? Here are my suggestions...

ACCESSORIES

Here we're talking about bags, hats, belts and jewellery. Now, I'm pretty fond of this genre – who doesn't love bags? However, it's one that can get a little out of control. Accessories are the one thing that turn a plain white t-shirt and jeans into something spectacular, so the amount that we have on hand is going to differ depending on how decorated we like to be. I'd recommend going through and giving away any items that you haven't found yourself wearing in the past 12 months. Anything that's left, keep it and use it to jazz up your basics. I have a few different pairs of hoop earrings, a black belt, one straw fedora hat for summer and a knitted beanie for the winter, then I probably have about eight bags that cover all bases from large totes for travel to a little Chanel clutch that I will probably be buried with, and that's enough for me.

UNDERWEAR

I will admit that I'm probably not the best person to speak on this matter because the bra that I like to wear the most is actually coming apart at the seams. However, I'll try my best and I did recently get rid of all my hole-ridden socks and buy new ones, and it made me feel like a QUEEN. It shouldn't take hours, but tip out the contents of your underwear drawer and just be mindful about what goes back in. Bras that no longer fit or are falling apart? They gotta go (adding this in as a note to self). Pants that dig in or are just a bit ropey? Yep, out they go too. Socks with holes? BYE BYE. Make yourself a shopping list for any items that you need to re-stock, and then do so when your budget next allows.

PYJAMAS AND LOUNGEWEAR

MY FAVOURITE CATEGORY! Even before I began working from home and wearing pyjamas 24/7 for five days out of seven – sorry DPD guy! – I've always been a lover of comfortable clothing in the home. If you ever turn up unannounced then you can bet your bottom dollar I'll be wearing a t-shirt that looks like I stole it from my husband, and some tracksuit bottoms that if I don't diligently tie up at the waistband will promptly fall around my ankles. Clearing out your drawer follows the exact same method as carried out for your underwear: strip your stash of anything that's barely holding together at the seams, no longer fits or never gets worn. For some reason I find this category to be a real collector's magnet, but in theory we only need around four pairs – two for the cooler months, such as t-shirts with short or long sleeves and long trousers, and and two vest top and short combos that you can always chop and change with the others you own depending on the weather, but mainly for the summer months.

I never used to think that activewear was something that was worth investing in, but now I get it. I'm not saying that you have to spend a three-figure sum on a pair of leggings, but just a good-quality pair that don't dig in, ride up or down and aren't completely see-through when you open up your legs to stretch, are worth dishing out a little for. Go through all your kit and remove any items that are no longer fit for purpose: if they're torn, worn and not fixable, if they no longer fit/are too big, if they're just not practical and feel uncomfortable when you sweat – donate any from these last two categories, where possible. Then if you're lacking in any particular areas, make yourself a shopping list. Take how often you work out in a week, and then add one or two to that number so you never run out of fresh sporting goods. I try to work out four times a week, so make sure I have five sports bras, five leggings and five tops. Add two pairs of trainers into the mix - one for running (if that's your bag) and one for general gym stuff - and that's you sorted. Sportswear takes a couple of hours to dry after a wash, so don't feel like you need to have the whole Nike sports department in your drawers.

Now, this is a little bit of a tricky one, especially if you've reached that age where you have to go to weddings every other weekend and really don't want to be asked to go on another £350 hen do for the fifth time this year. I'd recommend finding your formal wear flow. Do you like a co-ord? Perhaps you're more of a jumpsuit gal? Is a tea dress more your thing? Maybe you like to mix it up and would be happy wearing all three? Personally, I feel most comfortable in jumpsuits, so have four in my wardrobe that I can rotate for these kinds of events, along with one floaty dress for when I fancy something a bit more summery. I find that a plain clutch and a printed clutch (leopard print OBVS), along with three pairs of heels – nude, black and printed (again leopard print) – leave me with enough options so I don't get bored.

How to store your clothing

Once you've edited your capsule to a place that you're happy with, presentation is key. After all, if you're still an active participant in the floordrobe philosophy, then getting ready in the morning is going to be just as much of a saga, just with fewer items in your pile. The wardrobe space in our current flat isn't great, so I've created a technique for organising my clothing in a way that lends itself to even the tiniest of nooks; don't feel defeated if you've yet to secure your dream of a walk-in wardrobe just yet. One day, ONE DAY!

CURRENT SEASON

With your current in-season capsule I'd suggest hanging whatever you can. It's the fastest way to put your clothes away neatly post-wash, and the easiest way of seeing what you own at a glance. If there's something particular that you've grown a rather large collection of, like t-shirts or jeans, then it might be best to fold and stack them on a shelf or in a drawer to free up some hanger space. I fold items of clothing so that they make a small rectangular shape, then I can stack them up and see everything in the one drawer – like books where you can see the spines. While we're on the topic of folding, heavy knitwear (and just knitwear in general) is best folded to hold its shape and avoid stretching. In my side of our IKEA number I fold and stack knitwear and t-shirts at the top, hang everything else, lay out shoes on the bottom (not ideal but I dry and clean them off before they go in), then have two drawers underneath: one for underwear and pyjamas and another for activewear. All my clothing is fair game for wearing every day, but if you do have a work wardrobe and a home wardrobe, then it might make sense to visually split the two and stick your work stuff at one end of the wardrobe, and your home stuff at the other.

OUT OF SEASON

For out-of-season clothing, under-bed storage is the ideal spot because every now and again a freak day of weather may cause you to dig out a camisole, or your thick and fluffy coat. Before you pack anything away, make sure all items are freshly laundered, or dry-cleaned if needed, and are in good condition with any repairs or alterations made. If under-bed storage isn't an option, then look for alternative solutions.

Those space-saving vacuum bags are a good option because they're not too expensive, are so darn fun to use, and pack down so slim they can be slid under or behind pieces of furniture if you're struggling for space. Or make use of any unused spots, like the inside of a suitcase. My personal set-up for my off-season capsule features two under-bed drawers – one for shoes (and paperwork, bizarrely), and another for the rest of my clothing. In the winter, as everything is bulkier – it's actually a workout trying to fit a faux-fur-lined parka jacket under the bed, let me tell you – I add any overflow items into a suitcase and am always pleasantly surprised whenever I go on holiday. *Oh look, my pair of Ugg boots that I wear way more often than I'd ever like to admit!*

Capsule wardrobe troubleshooting

There are some common misconceptions out there about capsule wardrobes, so let me just turn them all on their head for a minute and offer up some solutions.

IT'S AN EXPENSIVE PROCESS

The budget is completely up to you. If a new season drops in and you don't feel the need to add any items or your budget doesn't allow for that – no problemo. Get creative with what you've already got – something that is a huge part of the capsule wardrobe ethos anyway.

YOU DON'T HAVE ENOUGH SPACE FOR IT

A capsule wardrobe should mean that you free up some breathing space in there. Sure, a spot to store your out-of-season stock is ideal, but if that's not possible then split your wardrobe into two, so you only ever have one side of it in operation at one time.

IT'S TIME-CONSUMING

Yes, it can take a little time. I can't deny that – the seasonal review and re-stock can munch into hours. However, think of all the time you'll save scrolling. I like to make my purchases for my new season capsule within the first couple of weeks of getting into it, then I'll try and buy absolutely nothing until the next season rolls around, completely shutting down the need to check all my favourite fashion sites daily. So in the end you save time, especially when you factor in how easy it becomes to find an outfit in the morning. No more running for the bus and panting for five minutes in a stranger's face when you make it on.

How to maintain a capsule wardrobe

You know the old 'quality over quantity' saying that you've been using to justify why it makes sense to spend a small fortune on one 'ripe and ready' avocado instead of four little ones that are so hard they still feel like pebbles two weeks after purchase? Well, I feel like there is no situation that suits it better than buying clothing. Remember when you were younger and you'd stretch your Saturday-only pay packet into a shopping spree and a Pizza Hut buffet lunch? A £2 pair of sandals here, a brown boho three-tier skirt that cost less than your hourly rate (I was desperately trying to channel some Nicole Richie circa 2008 boho vibes). I wore the sandals for a season, but by the next summer the stitching had unravelled and holes had appeared in the soles. Whether the damage was down to my heavy stride or not, I now try to buy clothing that's built to last, and the 'quality over quantity' mantra rules over all other justifications when it comes to making purchases.

In an ideal world you'd buy an item and 25 years later it would still be in one piece, ready for you to wear. You would feel a slight smugness every time someone asked where it was from. However, that's not going to be the case for everything, especially clothing that we wear day-in day-out.

I aim for a mix of higher-end pieces that are worth splashing out on, and lower-end items that are just as good quality but will probably need replacing sooner...

SPLASH OUT ON:	SAVE ON:
Jackets, coats and any outerwear	Cotton t-shirts
Knitwear (especially on cashmere and wool pieces)	Denim
Boots and leather shoes	Summer shoes (sandals & espadrilles)
Tailoring (blazers and fitted trousers)	Any white tops (sweat marks and stains are hard to remove)
Basics that you'll return to season after season and things you wear all the time	Trend-led pieces and items you don't find yourself reaching for so often

In order to make the distinction between which garments fit into which category for you, I'd recommend not only keeping track of what you feel your capsule wardrobe is lacking, so that needs adding, but also doing the same with your most worn items too, so it's easy to decipher where you should prioritise when making investments. I keep track of this in a page in my Bullet Journal. As an example, here's a list that I made back in summer 2017:

SUMMER CAPSULE WARDROBE 2017

MOST WORN ITEMS:

- Gucci leather loafers
- Equipment tie-dye silk shirt
- Straw basket bag
- Plain t-shirts
- Topshop pale wash denim jeans

ITEMS STILL MISSING:

- Leather sandals
- Shorts, skirts & dresses
- Camisoles that actually fit and don't expose my nipples every 2 minutes

So you've worked out what you need, and you want to make sure you make the right purchase – but when it comes to quality, what exactly does that mean? It's not necessarily to do with price, as you might expect, and you should take into account these other factors before you buy or decide to keep something you've bought.

DURABILITY

We want items that wash well and are going to last. It's important that the garment is well made and isn't going to rip, or that the fabric doesn't ball up and pill away. See further down for how to assess quality and durability.

COMFORT

Practicality is key with clothing, so we don't want items that we feel we need to fuss with all day long. Look for smooth seams that don't aggravate the skin and waistbands, tailoring and cuffs that don't dig in.

FIT

If you're going to invest in an item then you want it to look high quality, and for that it needs to sit on the body as intended and move with your body.

Take your time. Instead of grabbing an item of clothing off the hanger, trying it on for five seconds in a clammy changing room and marching up to the till to do the deed, you need to think a little more about what you're buying. The same goes for if you've purchased an item online: take time by making sure it's durable, comfy and fits well, then pair it with other items from your wardrobe to see how versatile it will be. If it doesn't satisfy these categories, then return it.

How to assess quality

It's time to get up close and personal with your purchases and become your own quality-control officers. Get your trench coat and your magnifying glass out, ladies. Of course we need to do all the usual 'trying on' tests: sitting down, bending over, putting your arms up in the air, doing the Macarena, but to really assess quality we need to give it a visual once-over too. It's just about knowing what to look for, so here's a mini guide of what to check next time you're in shopping mode.

1: LOOK AT THE FABRIC

Turn the garment inside out and locate the tag to find the exact fabric composition:

LINEN

Just by having a large percentage of linen in it, the fabric should be pretty high quality as there are fewer discrepancies in the fabric overall. The linen shouldn't feel rough, and remember that it naturally wrinkles so make sure that's something that you wouldn't mind. Ball it up in your hand to see how that specific linen creases. Be careful if there are any major creases in it at the time of purchase, as deep wrinkles from folding or hanging incorrectly might be hard to get out.

COTTON

It's actually a good choice to shop from lower-end stores for cotton items because it's a cheap fabric to produce anyway. Higher-quality cotton is made from long fibres and you can check for this by making sure that it feels soft, that it's not pilling and that even if it's a pretty transparent garment, it doesn't let through a lot of light when you hold it up to daylight. Cotton is a great option during the summer because it's breathable and easy to care for.

SILK

Silk should feel soft to the touch, and if you rub the fabric between your fingers you'll feel warmth from it. Examine the lustre, as the colour of the surface should shift a little in the light, whereas lower-quality silks only reflect back a white sheen.

WOOL

It's a bit of a tricky one as there are so many types and lots of quality differences here, depending on how the wool has been made. However, the knitting of any wool item should be consistent and there shouldn't be any pilling on the fabric at the time of purchase (although this will happen over time). Bear in mind the softness and how it will feel against your skin throughout the day; for example, mohair can get a little scratchy whatever the level of quality, whereas well-made cashmere is soft and gentle to wear.

DENIM

Check the denim all over and look at the stitching and the seams, as both should be consistent and straight and not pull away when you try and stretch the fabric. Watch out for seams that twist – especially around the knees – on poorly made jeans. Thickness isn't an indicator of quality, though, and is more of a personal preference – although thicker styles will last longer and thinner ones that are cut with elastic in the fabric will be more prone to losing their shape.

LEATHER

Look for full-grain leather – you know that slightly bobbly texture that leather sometimes has? That's the highest-quality stuff that's going to wear best. Assess it closely to check that it's an inconsistent pattern and hasn't been printed on. Check how the pieces of leather have been attached too; strong seams are what you're looking for, fitting it together with glue is a major no-no.

There's not one rule for all when it comes to synthetic fabrics, as they each have their own characteristics, advantages and disadvantages in terms of use and care instructions. I'd suggest having a quick Google from the changing room once you've looked at the fabric label if you're unsure. And use your hands to guide you, making sure the fabric feels smooth and soft and holding it up to the light and gently stretching it to check the density of the weave (the thicker the better).

2: TURN IT INSIDE OUT

Once you've checked out the fabric, look at the seams that are joining it all together and make sure that there aren't any loose threads. Neat and straight seams are a sign of a higher-quality piece, and crooked and messy seams a sign of a lower-quality one – *simple.* Try to tug the fabric a little to make sure that all the seams are stable, and when you're wearing it all seams should lie flat and close to the body. If an item is patterned, a high-quality piece will match up the pattern at all the joins so that it looks like it's made from one piece of fabric, making the end result look super-sleek. Seriously, once you start looking out for that final point, you realise what a difference it can make to the finish of a garment. SO CHIC.

Not all pieces of clothing have a lining, but if they do it's a good sign. It makes it easier for you to slip in and out of, and protects the inner seams and outer fabric from all the funky things that your body excretes. Inspect it like you would the outer fabric (see above) and make sure that it has the same care instructions as the rest of the item, or else cleaning it is going to be a pain in the arse.

3: ASSESS THE DETAILING

Now it's time to get your magnifying glass in real close and check out the finer details of your possible purchase. Now, I always thought that pockets that are stitched closed are a sign of poor quality, but actually it's to give you the option of keeping them that way and having the garment sit close to your body, or opening them up yourself if you'd rather they function. GENIUS. Either way, the stitching should be neat and there should be no excess thread inside. Zips should open and close easily without sticking, and movement shouldn't cause the zip to open or gape at all. Buttons are the final thing to check and are an easy giveaway as to whether the item is well made or not. In high-quality pieces they are well secured and a spare button should be provided. Look closely too at the buttonhole to check that it's been reinforced, and you can't see any raw edges of fabric through the stitching.

Sure, it's a bit of a process, but by going through these checks you'll be able to spot a well-made piece that's low end, or a high-end piece where the manufacturers have cut corners, ensuring that you make smart purchases that aren't going to fall apart after one wash. Now you know what to look for, you can make informed decisions about what's worth it and what's worth leaving behind.

How I care for my clothing

So you've edited your clothing stocks down and you're left with the items that fit, the items that work with your style and the items that you love, which probably means that everything is getting more use than ever before. If you have less, you're wearing items more and that means that your laundry pile and washing cycles are bound to increase. It's not the sexiest of topics, but how you care for your clothing is a big part of the capsule wardrobe strategy, as the more TLC you give your garments the longer they are going to last – and that's the ultimate aim here. So swotting up on your clothing care techniques and reading up on clothing labels and what all those symbols mean is worth the faff. I promise.

The good thing is that once you've worked out how to wash a particular garment, the process of dividing up your washing basket becomes a simple one that you can do in approximately two minutes. Ok, the hand washing might take a bit longer and having to traipse to and from the dry cleaners monthly to pick up your laundered fancy bits is yet *another* errand to put on the list, but hopefully you'll never have to endure another shrunken, pink-dyed jumper that looks like it wouldn't even fit a Barbie doll.

Nine times out of ten, though, we know what we're dealing with and can bundle our clothing together for a big ol' wash that we could do with our eyes closed. I just make sure I split my clothing into two piles: one for lights and one for darks, and then wash each load with non-bio detergent, a slug of fabric softener (although avoid this step if you're washing activewear as it leaves behind a residue on lycra that can attract bacteria) and stick it on a 30°C quick-wash. We go for the fast setting because it only takes one hour instead of three so means we can get all the dark washing done in an evening, plus it's better for your water bill and the environment.

When it's done we avoid the tumble drier: one, because ours no longer works; and two, because it throws your clothes around a bit and I can never be bothered to sort out all the creases. Instead, we hang them up on a line and clothes horse, and give them a blast with the dehumidifier if the processes needs a bit of help. I iron whatever I can be bothered to (i.e. nothing), then hang and fold up the fresh items back in my wardrobe. However, for those slightly trickier fabrics that need a bit more attention – you know the ones that have laundry tags that are so long that you never want to wear them ever again without sticking sanitary towels under your armpits? – don't panic. I've got you covered…

Now hear me out here, because it's kind of gross, but my life has been changed since I bought some plain, thin t-shirts that can easily be worn under my cashmere jumpers and chunky knits without adding too much heat, therefore meaning that I just have to wash some cotton t-shirts instead of having to wash my wool and cashmere all the time. LIFE. CHANGING. When I do have to wash my jumpers, I take it case by case. If I've sweated a tonne, been somewhere smoky or the jumper cost me an amount that I never want my mum to find out, then I take it to the dry cleaners. If the jumper hasn't grown legs yet, but was still a hefty investment, I go down the cold hand wash at home route, using a cashmere-specific detergent and making sure I dry the garment flat and without too much pulling or tugging. If I'm feeling lazy then I'll pop it on a cool, woollens cycle in the washing machine, again with the right detergent, and pray for the best. Wool tends to be hardier than cashmere and so I default straight to the third option most of the time. I'd also recommend picking up a cashmere comb, which is perhaps the most relaxing thing to use ever. You know how a pumice gets rid of dry skin on your feet? This basically does the same over any pilling fabrics, and it's so darn handy.

Over the years I have made a hobby of completely messing up silk shirts, so let's just say that my method here is a tried-and-tested one FOR SURE. There are some silk shirts in the world that just aren't made for washing. Check the laundry instructions, but if it says that it's dry clean only and the texture of the silk is brushed in a way that creates a sheen in the fabric which changes direction when you wipe your hand over it, then leave it to the professionals. Silk shirts that don't fit that criteria I put in the washing machine on a cool, short wash for delicates. I let them air-dry (silk should never be tumble dried), before giving them a once-over with a clothing steamer that makes me feel like a Vogue intern.

There's a bit of a debate on the best way to care for denim – some use a special detergent and some say you should wash it as little as possible, if ever, which to me sounds like a UTI just waiting to happen. I try and hit somewhere in the middle. I wash my denims in with my normal loads, but I do make sure they're always turned inside out before I sling 'em in, and try to wash them as infrequently as I can get away with, to try to prolong their shape and wash.

If a dry-clean-only piece falls into one of the three previous categories and doesn't seem too delicate, then *sometimes* I'll chance it and go down the hand-wash route. Firstly, I test it with water on a small patch in an inconspicuous area to see what happens, and secondly, it's something that I only attempt with things that I wear regularly, like shirts and knitwear. If it's more of an occasionwear piece like a dress or a jumpsuit, I'll take the sting and hop down to the dry cleaners, as they have a magic way of making things look like brand new. If I've only worn the item for a short period of time and it's still pretty fresh, I find that a once-over with the clothing steamer does the trick.

The Edit

When you compare it with other topics that we've covered in
An Edited Life, a capsule wardrobe seems like an insignificant
piece of the puzzle; it really isn't just a random piece of sky,
but nor is it a corner piece. It is, however, an integral piece of
the puzzle, and the puzzle just wouldn't be complete without
it. You don't have to go the whole hog, with seasonal updates
and keeping notes in your diary, but even if this chapter has
spurred you on to get rid of items that are no longer fit for
purpose, or no longer fit full stop, then you'll reap the benefits
of owning a cut-down and edited selection of clothing.
If you're still undecided, then why not try it on for size?
Even just the initial clear-out steps are a sure-fire cathartic
exercise, and we could all do with having a cold, hard look at
our spending habits and the wares that we accumulate. Along
with a clear-out, you're on the road to being a laundry pro –
and your whites and delicates will thank you for that, I'm sure.

We're just finetuning now – we're almost there and hopefully
this step is one where you'll be able to notice a difference
immediately. Once you've begun to organise all other aspects
of your life, it seems only logical to apply the same beliefs to
the part of us that plays a big role in how we present ourselves
to others and to the outside world. When you're indoors,
though, it's *all* about the elasticated waistbands and fluffy
slippers, and, speaking of indoors, the home and the day-
to-day running of it is the last topic on the cards here. From
cleaning routines to tidy tips from your resident neat freak
(that's me), we're only one step away from an edited life…

Running a home

Your belongings have been streamlined, so it's now time to incorporate a cleaning routine into your day to create a home environment that's the perfect habitat for you and your edited life.

I should preface this chapter by saying that I do not have children. I do not have pets. I do not have a messy husband. So when you combine these three things together, running a household is not currently a particularly taxing task. We do a weekly clean. We pay the bills. We do washing. We do a food shop. We watch cooking videos from the *Bon Appétit* YouTube channel in bed before we go to sleep. Oh yes, *it's a real riot over here*. So those with kids, over-excited dogs and/or an OH who thinks that taking the bin out every fortnight is too often, feel free to give yourself a pat on the back, lightly breeze over the chapter and prod holes in my methodology. I'm going to give it to you anyway, despite my lack of gritty experience. After all, I have managed to survive a complete home renovation and a wedding day reception that we held in our two-bed flat, so I do know a thing or two about post-reno deep cleans and how to get spilt Aperol spritz out from a cream wool carpet (Dirtbusters Stain Remover from Amazon is a gift sent down from heaven).

This chapter is the final one covered in *An Edited Life* because it's all about those little finishing touches that bring everything together. A capsule wardrobe is just a bit grim if you've got dust bunnies collecting in the corners of your closet. Meal planning is great, but if you never get round to doing a food shop then your list will remain unticked. Trust me – a Sunday lie-in is all the sweeter in fresh sheets. Running your household operations as a slick business that silently churns away in the background, demanding an amount of elbow grease but little brainpower, is the cherry on top of it all.

It takes a bit of time to put into place and develop these habits that work best for you, your home and all co-inhabitants, but once clicked into place it'll free up time so you're not spending your Sunday removing years old debris from your oven. I thought that budgeting was the least sexy part of this book, but say hello to the grand finale that's all about... *cleaning*.

Now, I wouldn't say that I'm someone who *loves* cleaning, but I am a direct descendant of a woman who hoovered her nineties bedroom carpet with such precision that it left a perfectly spaced out sheen on top so you could see where the vacuum had been forced backwards and forwards. *Shout-out to my mum!* I'm not fond of the legwork, but I enjoy the end result, and really that's the whole point. Dusting is balls and I would like to never have to take out a bin ever again, but, along with other household chores, these create a clean and tidy home environment that should help you to relax and feel more zen when you open the door.

We all know that we feel better when our homes are clean and organised, but these mental and psychical benefits have been scientifically proven. A 2010 study published in the *Personality and Social Psychology Bulletin* found that women who described their living spaces as 'cluttered' were more likely to be depressed and fatigued than those who found their homes to be 'restful' and 'restorative'. In 2011, researchers at Princeton University found that clutter decreased participants' ability to focus on a task, and a survey conducted by the National Sleep Foundation found that 75% of people say that they get a better night's sleep when their sheets are freshly washed. At its core, a well-run and edited home environment is an act of self-love; by taking pride in the space around you, you are demonstrating to yourself that you deserve to be in a beautiful and well-maintained environment. YOU DESERVE IT! Need more convincing as to why having a household routine is a good idea? This should push you over the edge:

- Not so many discoveries of hairs that are possibly pubic.

- Your home smells good, feels inviting and you don't have to wipe all the dust off the TV with your dressing gown sleeve before you watch it.

- No need to panic next time your parents arrive unannounced, as your home is already rocking five-star-hotel cleanliness vibes.

- Less time spent cleaning overall. YES, REALLY!

The last one got you, didn't it? You see, for cleaning I believe in
the opposite of my capsule wardrobe mantra. For clothing I preach
the quality over quantity approach, whereas for cleaning I vote that
quantity, along with a decent level of quality, is where it's at. Little and
often. There are few household tasks that I partake in daily, but a fair
amount that I do weekly and I feel that keeping on top of chores in this
way results in faster 'micro' cleans instead of those deep ones that you
have to do when you haven't hoovered in YONKS and it takes hours.
More is less, once you add it up overall: it's just about creating these
habits and nailing them into your schedule so that you automate and
complete them without even thinking about it. Here's how to spend
less time cleaning and more time doing the 1,943,487 activities that are
more enjoyable…

Let's get clean *yawn*

How you clean will depend on who you live with…

IF YOU LIVE ON YOUR OWN

Fab. Your cleaning is your responsibility and your responsibility only,
so take ownership of it and if you fancy doing the hoovering at 10pm
on a Tuesday then go ahead, and I'm pleased I'm not your downstairs
neighbour.

IF YOU LIVE WITH YOUR MATES

It's probably best to communicate and create some kind of schedule,
even if it does make you look like a massive square. It doesn't have
to be laminated and stuck on the fridge, but everyone needs to be on
the same page. I've heard of weekly rotas working where each week
you have your own set tasks and then you swap for the following week
on rotation, or sometimes it's better to assign one person the job of
cleaning one week and take it in turns weekly, which can work well if
you're all pretty busy and often find yourselves away.

IF YOU LIVE WITH YOUR FAMILY

The chances are that you already have some kind of cleaning
agreement set between all of you and ingrained from your two-
decades-plus of living together. If you feel like you're not pulling
your weight, then step up to the plate and take on more cleaning
responsibilities. You never know, this good deed might give you more
swing next time there's a tussle for the TV remote.

IF YOU LIVE WITH YOUR SIGNIFICANT OTHER.

How you splice up the household running order is something to discuss, as you're in it for the long term. The secret to a happy relationship? Aiming as close to a 50:50 split where fair and possible, given both of your schedules, so that you're not angrily thrusting a bleach-soaked toilet brush down the loo. We split the actual cleaning part into two, with Mark taking on the kitchen and bathroom and me owning the rest of the flat. Sure, sometimes it doesn't break down that way if one of us is travelling, but on the whole we try and split as much as possible. If the idea of cleaning the bathroom weekly makes you want to curl up and fall asleep in the tub, then rotate tasks so you get to mix things up. If you're both pitching in equally then you can save your energy for bickering about more important things, like where to spend Christmas this year and who last filled up the car with petrol.

Once you've worked out how to split the tasks, you need to identify what it is that you actually need to do and how often you need to do it. Maybe you've got cleaning bossed already and just need to solidify some sort of schedule into your routine, or perhaps you feel like your cleaning stash is lacking and you don't know your Mr Muscle from your Toilet Duck? The next section should have you covered for both of these conundrums and more.

Your household schedule

You know the drill. By doing a handful of tasks daily, it means that there's not so much that needs doing weekly. By doing a speedy clean weekly, there's not two inches of dust to cut through the next time you get round to it. It's a domino effect, and by roughly following the guide opposite they'll become things you do without really thinking about it, listening to a cracking podcast you have on in the background instead. Here's how I recommend breaking it down...

DAILY	WEEKLY	BI-YEARLY	YEARLY
Make your bed in the morning.	Do your laundry (or more often if required, although we do two/three loads weekly).	Give your blinds a proper dust and clean.	If you have curtains, give them a clean.
Tidy up after dinner by washing up your cookware or sticking it all in the dishwasher and give the surfaces a quick wipe.	Change your bedding and wash all your towels.	Deep-clean the oven and make sure everything is looking good with your dishwasher and washing machine.	Clean your windows from the inside and organise for a window cleaner to clean them from the outside if it's not possible for you to do so.
Keep an eye on the bins and take out the rubbish/recycling if needed.	Give all your surfaces, belongings, picture rails and skirting boards a quick dust (start high and work down low).	Do a deep hoover; cleaning under and behind furniture, paying special attention to around the bed and mattress.	Defrost the freezer (you may need to do this more or less frequently than once a year).
Put things back in their home as you use them to avoid having to do a big tidy-up at the end of the week.	Hoover all floors and carpets and then mop floors if necessary.	Rotate your mattress (and flip if necessary – Google to see if your mattress needs that tool), every three months to a year.	
	Clean the kitchen and bathroom.		
	See what's going on in your fridge; meal plan for the next week, write a list and organise a food shop.		

These are the household hygiene puzzle pieces, so schedule them in around your routine. The daily to-dos are now ones that I do automatically; if they are things I keep on top of, they take up such a short amount of time. The bulk of the weekly stuff we like to do on a Saturday morning, just so it's out of the way and we can enjoy the rest of our free time at the weekend. I do, however, tend to do laundry on a Monday (because as it transforms our home into a wet clothing museum until it's all dry, it doesn't then flap around in the faces of guests, who tend to visit more towards the end of the week and the weekend) and a food shop too, as that works better with our meal planning. The bi-yearly stuff sort of kicks in on its own because the oven starts to create a funky waft that signifies that it's time to give it a good wash down, and we start to wonder if the carpets underneath the bed might just be permanently grey. For the yearly cleaning pointers it might make sense to put reminders in your calendar as they're not the most memorable things that you'll keep track of in your mind, unless there's a 'When I'm cleaning windows' nude exposure situation that's burnt into your brain. Now you need to assemble your cleaning arsenal.

Your cleaning kit

You need the right tools to get the job done. I still remember trying to get lipstick that I'd smooshed into a carpet out with just water and some tissue paper and perspiring madly because I knew I was in deep shit. Note to my 10-year-old self: Don't steal your mum's lipstick and then drop it. FOOL. The supermarket aisle can make it seem like you need to drop a small fortune and have enough space in your cupboards for 27 different types of cleaning agents, but I reckon that with the following in your kit, you'll be covered for around 99% of cleaning, spillage and stain situations:

ALL-PURPOSE ANTI-BACTERIAL CLEANER

If you've got yourself a bottle of this then you're all good. Use it for everything, from bathrooms to kitchens and bedside tables. I am rather partial to the Method brand because they scent them in a way that smells like you've been burning the fanciest candle you own for 24 hours straight.

TOILET CLEANER

Make sure you've got some hefty stuff because a lot goes on down there. I use my all-purpose cleaner for the exterior and then something bleach-based for the interior. It's not the nicest thing to keep in your stash, but it does come in handy when you've somehow managed to mark your brand new white sink with eyebrow dye, let me tell you that.

GLASS CLEANER

If you try using anything aside from glass cleaner on a mirrored surface you'll be spending the rest of the day seeing a whole host of smears in various different patterns every time the light changes. It's an impossible game of catch-me-if-you-can. If you have any fancy schmancy surfaces then it might be worth picking up a wood and/or stone cleaner too, as those can often require some personalised TLC.

FLOOR CLEANER

You could dilute your all-purpose cleaner to create a mix that's suitable for your floor and doesn't break the bank, although I have one that doesn't require diluting and shoots right out onto the floor from the bottle, which makes things quick and easy. If you have carpets make sure you have a carpet stain remover too because, you know… *red wine*.

OVEN CLEANER

This might seem like a fair amount of specific cleaners, but if there's one type of specific cleaner you need, it's for your oven. That shit is cooked on in there and without a formula that's designed for that, paired with some vigorous scrubbing, it ain't ever coming off.

MICROFIBRE CLOTHS

These cloths have changed my life, and entered it thanks to a recommendation from my friend Sally who has the cleanest home out of everyone that I know. Buy a pack that contains different colours so that you can colour-code and use them exclusively in certain areas, then there will be no chance of using your loo cloth in the kitchen. They negate the need to use so much kitchen roll and completely take out the need for wipes, are easy to clean, dry quickly and don't need replacing that often.

DUAL-SIDED SPONGE

A bit of a boring purchase, but having something that's gently abrasive comes in very handy whenever you need to give something a good scrub – like your bath tub, sink, kitchen hob and oven.

FEATHER DUSTER

My feather duster brings me great joy as it has an extendable arm and a fully malleable fluffy top bit, which means that I can manipulate it into whatever shape I want to reach every single nook and cranny in our home. Have a look online and find yourself one, because it makes dusting an activity that doesn't cause you to put your back out every time you go to reach for the high bits.

MOP

I prefer those sponge-top ones as they dry more quickly than a traditional mop, or if you're feeling real fancy you could buy yourself one of those designs that has a spritzer on the handle and that sprays the floor with whatever cleaner you fill it with. GENIUS.
I'd recommend a dustpan and brush too, for cleaning up any broken glass or small dusty spillages, and to avoid always having to get the hoover out.

VACUUM CLEANER

After years of using one that was provided by our landlord and was the reason why we still had leftover Christmas tree pine needles stabbing our feet in late August, I'll still never forget the day that we invested in a hoover that wasn't £20 and it changed our lives. Research (Which? and Mumsnet are great), invest, make sure it's got a decent warranty on it and say goodbye to every single speck of dust that your shit vacuum cleaner has missed for the past two years.

It looks like a lot when it's written down, but mop and vacuum cleaner aside, it's nothing that won't fit under the sink with the rest of your 'I have no idea where else to store this?' supplies, which for me includes napkins and hot water bottles. If you're struggling to find a home for your vacuum cleaner, I'd recommend buying a compact style and then storing it behind an open door if you're low on large cupboard space.

So you've worked out your routine and checked off your supplies, but how else can you help make this household shit even easier? I have some final tips tucked up my sleeve...

Sometimes our routines don't always go to plan *eyes up the golf-ball-sized piece of fluff in the corner of the bathroom that could be dust or hair, or I'm not sure that I want to know*. Of course, the once-a-month 'I am not your mother!/I can't be arsed with this!' hormone-driven huff can always be predicted to the exact day as I stomp around the flat finding anything and everything to nitpick at, but with zero energy to do it myself. *Isn't Mark a lucky lad?* But often it's not an ovary-induced rage and subsequent slump that causes our cleaning routines and habits to run off the rails. Instead it's a combination of factors: time, travel, a lack of inspiration when it comes to meal planning, an influx of new items that I have no idea where to put, or sometimes a CBA attitude that just won't budge. In those cases it's time to bring in the special measures to get things back up to scratch…

DO YOU FEEL LIKE YOU JUST DON'T HAVE TIME? I actually really enjoy cooking and I'm partial to a good dusting session sometimes. However, when time on the clock feels like a laughable concept then I'm down for some household automation. Eating crap because you haven't got time to think up meal plans and do a shop? Can't remember the last time you cleaned? Keep running out of loo roll and forgetting to buy more? The tweaks offered below are all easy to incorporate and there's no shame in simplifying things for yourself or asking for help if it's something that fits in with your budget and means that you aren't having to scrub the bath when you get home at 9pm. Instead do this:

- Order yourself a weekly meal or veg box and schedule in a supermarket shop to be delivered to your door.

- Organise for a cleaner to pop round weekly while you're at work for the rest of the month until your weekends calm down and you can get back into your routine.

- Keep a shared grocery shopping list on your phone with the rest of your household that you can update immediately when you realise you're running low on food or household supplies.

BEEN ON HOLIDAY AND BEEN THROWN OFF KILTER? We travel a fair amount, which is both glorious and makes my stomach churn, because turbulence makes me clench my butt cheeks like nothing else. I have the packing side of things down, but upon my return I'm about as useful as a waterproof towel. I'm tired, I'm frazzled and all I want to do is eat pizza while side-eyeing my unopened suitcase. So I have a couple of strategies to make walking back though the front door as painless as possible.

- Before you go on holiday, get all remaining laundry done, as you can bet your bottom dollar that you'll have about eight loads to do when you get back.

- Make sure that a supermarket online shop is being delivered first thing the next morning after you arrive home (I never do it for that evening in case we're delayed) to avoid having to eat tinned goods until you have the energy to buy food.

- Order a food box delivery for the day of your return too, or ensure that there's something in the freezer to stop you from ordering takeaway on the night you get back when you've no doubt just eaten pizza, bread and pasta for a number of days (aka HEAVEN).

- Wash the sheets and put on fresh bedding before you leave for holiday, so your bed/cloud is ready and waiting for your return.

NEVER HAVE TIME TO COOK? I go more in-depth into this in the **Self-care** chapter where I mention meal planning, but feeding your freezer is a lesson that I learnt from my grandma, and is a simple step that often comes in *real* handy. Growing up we were big into batch cooking and storing the leftovers in the freezer, and it's still something that I like to do monthly now if I can. Back from holiday and nothing to eat? Check the freezer. Your family invited themselves over for dinner and you haven't got time to go to the supermarket? Check the freezer. Feeling lazy AF and don't want to move? You get the gist.

Spend an hour whipping up some fresh goods that are on the turn into some kind of stew, soup or pasta sauce.

Double or triple a recipe that you like and add the leftovers into individual Tupperware boxes in the freezer (my mum uses leftover butter and ice-cream cartons for this).

Take any herbs, chilli or garlic that are about to go off, slice them up and sprinkle into an ice-cube tray. Fill each ice cube up with oil, freeze and then pop out and use in cooking when needed.

STRUGGLING TO KEEP THINGS TIDY? There is one secret to having a tidy space (aside from the fact that I don't have kids) – *everything has a home*. There's no such thing as mess if every item you own has its own spot where it lives. You're looking to home things in a way that looks like it's supposed to be there, and is organised in a way that makes it easy to access and find if required.

Next time you buy something, find a spot for it to go ASAP, and the whole shit-tip phase is dodged. It also gives you a blueprint to follow next time you have a tidy-up, so you don't waste time brandishing your new vase that you bought because Instagram ads told you to and wondering where the hell to put it.

Find a spot where it works as soon as you can, get posting your #InteriorInspo IG, and tidying your belongings becomes something that happens without you even realising.

LETTING IT ALL PILE UP? I'm sure that it will come as no surprise to you (I mean – you've made it this far!) that I feel most at peace when our home is neat, clean and tidy. SHOCKER, eh? But even if a stack of unwashed dirty dishes on the side doesn't give you heart palpitations like it does me, I'd still recommend giving your home a quick once-over before you go to bed. Now, I'm not talking about whipping around the vacuum cleaner here, but just having a little spruce, you know?

- Wash and put away everything you used to make dinner. Hang up any washing that's sitting in a damp pile. Unload your work bag of items you don't need for the following day. Clean up that fake tan disaster you had in the bathroom earlier that looks like something terrible happened with an Oompa Loompa in there.

- Do it pre-sleep so it means that when you wake up the following morning you don't need to waste any time with leftover chores, and can even add 10 minutes onto your alarm.

These titbits of advice aren't difficult to put into place; they are mechanisms that will help to get the wheels moving again and make any household goings-on that you're struggling with run with fewer avoidable speed-bumps. Who doesn't love a method that hacks the system? There may still be days when you're struggling to remember the last time you mopped the kitchen floor, and are rubbing pasta sauce stains off the tiles with your sock, but hey – you meal planned. However, there may be week-long stretches where you feel like you might be the next cover star for *Good Housekeeping*, and the more of those the better – for both your surroundings and your mental health.

The Edit

Hopefully this chapter tied all the beliefs of *An Edited Life* together with a big fat bow. Once you've sorted through all aspects of life organisation and ironed out any issues in the workplace, the home is the last cog to oil up. After cherry-picking the advice that you'd like to heed and applying it to your household, things should be running more smoothly than ever. You'll have been able to pin down a cleaning routine and divvy up the tasks between all occupants, including working out a way so that all those nooks and crannies that often go missed are getting a good scrub too. Your cleaning kit is ON FIRE thanks to the list on p.132; don't say I never give you anything. Whatever information you soak up and whatever you decide to spit out, there will always be moments when you're pondering if a tub of ice cream is a nutritious enough dinner, or you spot a fluff-/dust-/hair-ball on the floor which looks like actual tumbleweed – and when they happen we need to give ourselves a break. Holding down a steady home environment while juggling life and work in the mix isn't possible all the time. Remember, no one is perfect except for Ryan Gosling.

Ok, so you've had ALL THE INFORMATION delivered to you. So much. But how the hell do you put all this into practice? Perhaps you've dipped in and out of the book and applied methods as you've worked through the chapters? Or maybe you were saving the 'doing bit' till you got to the end? There's a chance that you've got to this point and never want to think about organisation ever again. For that I sincerely apologise and I hope that you enjoy how pretty this book looks among your teetering book pile that towers over your bedroom. For the rest of you, here's how to put *An Edited Life* into practice...

AN EDITED

HOME

CHECK LIST

- [ ] Schedule time over the coming weeks and months to streamline your belongings using the F.U.L.L. method. Add these dates to your diary to give them priority and make sure that you're free to complete what you've set out to do.

- [ ] Give your sentimental belongings the F.U.L.L. treatment too.

- [ ] Create a capsule wardrobe and test out the technique for a whole season, only making purchases where necessary and avoiding impulse buying by always shopping with a list.

- [ ] Learn how to care for your clothing properly, making a trip to the dry cleaners and visiting the tailor if any items need altering or repairs.

- [ ] Organise a cleaning schedule for your household that includes tasks that need ticking off daily, weekly, bi-yearly and yearly.

- [ ] Beef out your household cleaning stash with any bits that you're lacking so you're ready to tackle the full spectrum of stain-removing dilemmas.

AN EDITED LIFE

THE ACTION PLANS

So it's almost time for me to belt out the chorus of that karaoke classic 'End Of The Road' by Boyz II Men, because it's time for me to tie up *An Edited Life* with a big fat bow.

I appreciate that I have given you ALL THE INFORMATION, so I thought that it might be helpful to drop in before I go and leave you with some ideas of how to incorporate into your home and work lives everything that I've shared.

I'm arming you with three plans of action over three different time periods, based on whether you'd like to edit over a weekend, a month or a three months.

Here's how to slot it all together.

Important things to remember

The plans in this section are nothing more than a guide to demonstrate how to piece together all the aspects of life, work and home organisation that I've covered, so nothing is set in stone here. If the weekend edit takes you a week? BRILL. If you fancy giving some practices a try for two months? SURE. Adapt things as you go, work the ideas into your life as you see fit and keep these things in mind:

- Starting is the painful bit, and once you get going you will begin to pick up pace. So make a start sooner rather than later. Even just putting one tip into action is better than nothing.

- Applying these habits and routines to your life isn't a one-off thing, but a constant process that requires editing as time passes. This doesn't mean that it needs to be all-consuming, more that you shouldn't be afraid of things going off in a different direction, or sometimes needing a bit more TLC.

- Aside from snippets that I've harvested from friends and family, the majority of methods that I've spoken about in here are all things that have worked out for me – and I'm just one Ryan-Gosling-obsessed, Virgo-vibing person in this big ol' world. So cherry-pick, tweak and apply what you feel like you need a helping hand with, and feel free to ignore the rest. I am well known for my waffling.

You ready to get the ball rolling? Here's how I'd suggest slotting *An Edited Life* into your life…

THE WEEKEND EDIT

- Take charge of your calendar situation and complete the quiz for whether you're a digital or paper planner from the **Sort your diary out** chapter. Add in your holidays, meetings and deadlines for the next 12 months and plan in your workouts and social events for the week ahead.

- Start thinking about your budget. The first step is to get familiar with your finances, so log into your online banking and do that EVERY DAY for the next week.

- Set yourself a meal plan for the week ahead. Work out what meals you need for each day, find recipes to cook for dinner and nutritious but speedy breakfast and lunch options, write out a shopping list and head to the supermarket (or do an online order if you're struggling for time).

- Turn to the **How to plan your working day** chapter and write a plan up for the week ahead along with daily to-do tasks.

- Vow to implement at least one time-saving technique during the upcoming working week, cribbed from the **How to get tasks done** chapter.

- Make a start on your streamlining journey by scheduling in when you plan to go through and edit your belongings in each of your rooms over the next few weeks.

- Give your home a good clean and tidy in preparation for the week as per the tips in the **Running a home** chapter.

- If you fancy testing out a capsule wardrobe, start the process by following the steps in the **How to build a capsule wardrobe** chapter.

THE MONTH-LONG EDIT

- Take your calendar to the next level. Along with adding in all your everyday bumf, make a note of birthdays and present-buying reminders, colour-coordinate your paper calendars, and if you're using a digital one, why not try having two calendars – one for your personal stuff and one for work? #Balance – quite literally.

- Get into the routine of checking your bank balance a couple of times a week, refer to the **Money** chapter for a template on how to set up a budgeting spreadsheet, and over a month track exactly what's coming in and what's going out of your account.

- Amp up your self-care. Once a week – even if it's just for 30 minutes – schedule in some time for you. Whether you want to sing your heart out in the shower to ABBA, or just want to read a book, do something that eases the weight on your shoulders for a moment.

- Read through the meal-planning section of the **Self-care** chapter and have a think about what would work best for your household, then roll with it and automate as much as you can to make life easier for yourself. That might be creating your own master list of recipes so you don't spend hours trawling though books, or saving all your online shopping favourites to lists so that they're easy to re-add next time you make an order.

- Set yourself the aim of working out twice a week for the whole month. Perhaps it's a power-walk round the block, or a yoga class you've always wanted to give a go. Whatever the activity – get your sweat on. Make yourself a tickable timetable and keep it pinned up in a high-traffic area of your home.

- Give yourself a goal to achieve by the end of the month, and use the **Creating goals & your future plans** chapter for advice on how to do this. It could be anything – work, life, home, whatever – just something to work your goal-setting muscle. Remember to make it S.M.A.R.T.

- Take a Friday evening or Monday morning to tidy up your workspace, as per the method set out in the **Organise your workspace** chapter.

- Tune in to your own personal energy levels as per the **How to plan your working day** chapter, and work out where your natural peaks and troughs are during your shift. Take a note of these and use this information when it comes to scheduling your week.

- A month is a decent length of time to properly tackle your inbox. Set up folders, delete messages you no longer need and get yourself into a routine with an inbox rule (e.g. only checking your inbox three times a day).

- Set yourself a room-by-room streamlining schedule and follow the F.U.L.L. method from the **How to streamline & organise your home** chapter. Depending on your plans for the month, you should be able to sift through at least 50% of your home, if not the whole thing. YEAH!

- Follow the steps in the **How to build a capsule wardrobe** chapter and give your remaining clothing some TLC; learn how to take care properly of the fabrics you own, and make any necessary repairs or alterations.

- Sort out your cleaning kit and set some time aside to give your home a head-to-toe clean, tackling everything that's on the schedule from the **Running a home** chapter, then adding in bi-yearly or yearly reminders for when big tasks next need doing.

THE THREE-MONTH EDIT

Three months is a decent amount of time to really get into budgeting. After tracking your spending, begin to get familiar with spreadsheets and follow the steps for creating one in **Money** chapter. Start to put the year-round and seasonal saving tips into practice.

Complete at least one digital detox during this period. *Like it?* Make a deal with yourself to complete them more often.

Along with meal planning and organising a weekly food shop, make sure you have your kitchen essentials *down*. Treat yourself to a new cookbook too, and challenge yourself to make some new recipes.

Set yourself up with an official workout routine and follow my tips from the **Self-care** chapter so that you actually stick to it. Don't be afraid of trying something new and mixing your routine up.

This a great length of time to really dig deep and think about your long-term goals. Work through the exercises in the **Creating goals & your future plans** chapter, and aim to solidify some long-term goals that you'd like to achieve; filter them down into action points that you can work into your weekly plans.

Ensure that your workspace is clean, tidy, free from paper and organised in such a way that it's most functional for you and your needs. Incorporate any additional storage items and remove anything from your immediate area that doesn't get used at least weekly.

Routines and habits sewn into your working day can be great time-savers, so have a set way that you write your to-do list, templates for email replies and a designed reply time for anything in your inbox. Make your own rules that actually make sense to follow, and that allow you to be even more efficient with your working hours.

Read through the 'flow' section of the **How to get tasks done** chapter and see how you can apply it to your own tasks.

Complete the streamlining process of all your belongings in every single room (even the sentimental stuff) and give every item you own the F.U.L.L. treatment. Sell what you can, donate and recycle the rest if possible and wave goodbye to all that shit you didn't need.

Try a full season of the capsule wardrobe. Familiarise yourself with indicators of quality in clothing, make mindful purchases (never shop without a list!) and look for inspiration of how to re-wear and recycle instead of buying new things on an impulse. Keep notes of your most frequently worn items and what you feel like you are lacking in. Use this information to prepare for the season ahead.

Tidy out your cleaning kit and fill the gaps of anything that you were missing. Complete a full-home deep-clean and then give one of the tips from the **Running a home** chapter a go. Maybe you fancy feeding your freezer? Or would you like to incorporate the tidy tip that cuts your tidying down by at least half?

Whatever points you decide to action, I hope they lead to you feeling like you have your shit just a *little* bit more together. Whether you take the whole 'quality over quantity' mantra on board, or start to say no and begin to respect your own schedule, I'm pretty confident that by heeding just a handful of the titbits that I've sprinkled throughout these chapters you'll begin to treat yourself with the kindness that you deserve, and ultimately end up with more time on the clock to do more of whatever makes you happy, and *that's* the end goal of all this malarkey.

One final thing...

Human beings are not perfect. We f-up. We're messy. We're emotional. We're all over the shop sometimes. So while I've proposed a set of suggestions here that we can all benefit from incorporating into our lives, no matter how much tweaking or editing we apply, occasionally it all goes tits up – even if you're an author of a book about life organisation. Here's a non-exhaustive list of some ironic things that happened during the writing process of *An Edited Life*.

- I developed an addiction to Candy Crush which I liked to play in bed before I went to sleep. I've now reached triple-digit levels and enjoy conversions with other Candy Crushers (shout-out to Millie!).

- Speaking of sleep, I began to really enjoy lie-ins, in a way that I never have done before. Wherever I could fit them in. I woke up to the doorbell thanks to the postman. I worked from bed. I went to bed late and woke up late and felt unproductive because of it.

- I ate a lot of crisps. And cookies. One time I did an UberEats order for a lunchtime McDonald's after I got back from Pilates. LOLZ.

- I went a whole month without going to Pilates and lost the ability to touch my toes. When I returned I had to hold back a happy tear because I felt like such a loser for not prioritising something that makes me and my tight hamstrings feel so good.

- I made a lot of Net-a-Porter orders. I returned a lot of Net-a-Porter orders, but there were some serious wardrobe investments made during this time that I'm not sure were strictly necessary.

The whole work/life balance thing? Yeah I fudged that up. I danced all night with my pals and then worked on a Sunday. I didn't bother my parents half as much as I usually do, which I'm sure they were secretly happy about. I cancelled dinners, meetings and didn't make it to family meet-ups as my time-management and priorities were in a spin.

I missed calls. I forgot to reply to messages. I was late to meetings. *'I'm so sorry, I'm running 10 minutes late!'* was my new version of being 10 minutes early.

The deadline for this book coincided with one of my busiest months, and I juggled brand work, recording a podcast, a newsletter, two trips abroad and trying to finish a 80,000-word book with regular weekly videos and thrice-weekly blog posts – and you know what? I felt overwhelmed. My planning was off. My to-do lists would remain unticked, and no matter what I did I still felt like a hamster in a wheel that wasn't going anywhere.

I ignored my own advice and didn't leave the house for three days. It culminated in me being so bored and procrastinating so badly that I called up the hairdresser's and went for a drastic chop, exiting the salon with about 65% of my original hair.

You see? But somehow among all these habits that aren't exactly aligned with *An Edited Life* I still managed to have one of my best years yet. I wrote a book. I travelled to some amazing places. I kept my blog and YouTube updated with new content. I made memories. I laughed. I cried because I'd drunk too much Whispering Angel and I just love my best mates *sooooo* much (LOLZ). I still held down a budget, a plan, a schedule, a capsule wardrobe, worked on my goals and ate considerably less takeaway pizza than the previous year. Maybe I wasn't as hot on to-do lists as I had previously been and I probably could have done a better job at keeping on top of a cleaning schedule. But as I've said approximately 476 times in this book, it's all about selecting what feels right for you at this exact moment, and that's exactly what I did. I edited my life, my work and home to a place that allowed me to be organised and efficient and free up as much time as possible to do the things in life that make me happy.

You're the pen, life's the paper and now you have the crib sheet on how to edit out the crap and leave in the good bits. It's time to be your own editor.

Resources

Further reading and research for an edited life…

PRINT-OUT PDFS AVAILABLE AT THEANNAEDIT.COM:

- How to Create a Budget Worksheet
- Meal Prep Planning & Shopping List Worksheet
- Fitness Routine & Goal Planner
- Weekly Planning Worksheet
- How to Build a Capsule Wardrobe Worksheet
- Holiday Packing Guides (both for cabin-bag-only trips & longer breaks)

WEBSITES:

INTOTHEGLOSS.COM // A website that is basically beauty-related self-care fodder. Whenever I'm in the mood to do some pampering, this is where I head for inspiration.

MONEYSAVINGEXPERT.COM // Ah come on – *you must have heard of this one?* It does what it says on the tin, offering unbiased, practical financial advice on a whole host of matters.

THEFINANCIALDIET.COM // a slightly more visually pleasing offering than the previous money-related recommendation, but equally helpful; written by women, for women.

THEELGINAVENUE.COM // For advice on productivity, business, relationships, careers – a bit of everything. Monica posts fab tips and methods that are so easy to implement.

THEWWCLUB.COM // A great hub for business advice from cool women who are doing cool shit. Big love for the free print-out worksheets too that are so handy, especially if you're self-employed.

UN-FANCY.COM // Where I originally discovered the concept of capsule wardrobes, so thanks for that Caroline! Here you'll find lots of info on the idea, along with practical posts on how she makes it work throughout the year.

PODCASTS:

WHERE SHOULD WE BEGIN? WITH ESTHER PEREL // It's like putting your ear up to the door of a room where a couple are having relationship counselling. There's something so therapeutic about listening to others work through their issues.

HAPPY PLACE WITH FEARNE COTTON // A feel-good podcast, where you'll take your headphones off and feel inspired, revived and ready to tackle the day.

GRIEFCAST BY CARIAD LLOYD // For a podcast that revolves around death and bereavement, it's surprisingly uplifting. A great one to listen to if you're struggling with the loss of a loved one.

CTRL ALT DELETE BY EMMA GANNON // Emma has on some cracking guests and often covers topics surrounding building a business, creativity and personal development.

HOW I BUILT THIS WITH GUY RAZ // Featuring high-profile interviews with founders of some of the most successful companies in the world, this is a fab podcast to whip out when your motivation levels are low.

TOOLS & APPS:

MONZO // This makes it so easy to manage your budget and see in an instant how your money is being spent, thanks to handy graphs and infographics.

HEALTH (THE IOS STEP TRACKER) // I use the health app that comes on iPhone to loosely keep an eye on how many steps I'm doing a day. It's not the most accurate, but it's good enough to use for a rough guide.

MOVEGB // An app where you can sign up and pay monthly to attend various different exercise classes in your area, so giving new moves a go is very easy.

HEADSPACE // A meditation app that is great to blast in your ears whenever you're not feeling the ticket. I find it works wonders when the pre-flight nerves kick in.

ASANA // The best productivity app for mobiles as it syncs up with the desktop site too and allows for full planning and time-management organisation.

BOOKS:

WHY SOCIAL MEDIA IS RUINING YOUR LIFE **BY KATHERINE ORMEROD** A critical look at how we use social media across all aspects of our lives; you'll definitely want to do a digital detox after a read.

EVERYTHING I KNOW ABOUT LOVE **BY DOLLY ALDERTON** Reading Dolly's experiences of her twenties is basically like chicken soup for the soul. Add it into your self-care routine ASAP.

RUNNING LIKE A GIRL **BY ALEXANDRA HEMINSLEY** If there's a book that can shove a rocket up your arse and make you want to run, or even just work out in general – it's this.

'THE BULLET JOURNAL METHOD' **BY RYDER CARROLL** A deep dive into the world of Bullet Journalling if you want to take your planning skills to the next level.

THE WORKING WOMAN'S HANDBOOK **BY PHOEBE LOVATT** Truly a handbook, in that it covers pretty much everything to do with the world of work – from how to design a pitch to asking for investment.

THE MULTI-HYPHEN METHOD **BY EMMA GANNON** If your goal for the next five years is to develop a business idea into a side-hustle then make sure you've got this on your bedside table.

LITTLE BLACK BOOK **BY OTEGHA UWAGBA** A speedy read that's easily devoured on a commute and a great refresher if you're feeling a little lacklustre about your career.

THE LIFE-CHANGING MAGIC OF TIDYING **BY MARIE KONDO** It's what got me started on this whole journey in the first place. If you fancy venturing into true minimalism then Marie's path is the one to take.

THE CURATED CLOSET **BY ANUSCHKA REES** Captured by the idea of a capsule wardrobe and want to know more? This book has everything you need to know, from style pointers to seasonal palette suggestions.

Acknowledgements

A massive thank you has to be said to anyone who has ever visited my corner of the Internet. So THANK YOU to all my readers who have ever stopped for a browse, left a comment, sent a tweet, written me an email or given one of my videos a thumbs up. I'm so lucky to have such a kind and dedicated audience and without you I wouldn't be writing the acknowledgements for my first ever book that's for sure. Your viewership and continued support means the world.

Thanks to my literary agent Abigail Bergstrom for believing in *An Edited Life* from day dot. Yours and Megan Staunton's feedback and encouragement has been invaluable and I feel so grateful to have two such cool cats in my life. Thank you to Susannah Otter at Quadrille Publishing – you were my publishing girl crush from the beginning and took my vision for this book to a place that I never even dreamt it could be. Thank you also to Emily Lapworth, Sara Lovejoy and Ruth Tewkesbury from Quadrille and Emily Burns at BrandHive – what a girl gang! Sending all the love to my managers Lucy and Millie for tentatively messaging 'R u ok hun?' WhatsApps whenever I went quiet. Thank you for always looking out for me and being my biggest cheerleaders.

A big shoutout to all my friends and family who were so supportive throughout this process, but especially Mel, Sammy-Jo, Lauren, Sally and Matt who allowed me to quiz them on their tidy tendencies. Thanks to Lily, my book writing mentor who held my hand throughout the whole thing.

A huge thank you to my husband Mark, who never complains or raises an eyebrow when I say I have just a *little* bit more work to do but actually mean three hours. Thank you for coming into my office and punching the air whenever I reached a word count milestone. You're the best. Then finally, to my parents – Jane and Steve. Thank you Mum for jumping up and down on the spot when I told you I had a book deal. You may be a hoarder but you sure are adorable. Thank you Dad for believing in this whole blogging thing from the beginning and helping me plot my big career move on our daily commutes up to London. Thanks for both making me tidy up my room every Saturday morning. You will forever and always be my favourite neat freaks.

PUBLISHING DIRECTOR Sarah Lavelle

COMMISSIONING EDITOR Susannah Otter

DESIGNER Emily Lapworth

PRODUCTION DIRECTOR Vincent Smith

PRODUCTION CONTROLLER Nikolaus Ginelli

Published in 2019 by Quadrille,
an imprint of Hardie Grant Publishing

Quadrille
52–54 Southwark Street
London SE1 1UN
quadrille.com

Cataloguing in Publication Data: a catalogue record
for this book is available from the British Library.

ISBN 978-1-78713-242-9

Printed in Italy